To Treg

Wishe

Best

THE ACOUSTICS OF
PERFORMANCE HALLS

SPACES FOR MUSIC FROM CARNEGIE HALL
TO THE HOLLYWOOD BOWL

THE ACOUSTICS OF PERFORMANCE HALLS

SPACES FOR MUSIC FROM CARNEGIE HALL

TO THE HOLLYWOOD BOWL

J. CHRISTOPHER JAFFE

FOREWORD BY LEO L. BERANEK

W. W. NORTON & COMPANY

NEW YORK • LONDON

To my late wife, Marcia Paris Jaffe, a talented musician, whose unerring ear was of valuable assistance at many concert hall openings and who shared with me an exciting musical acoustic adventure.

I would like to acknowledge the assistance and support of Bett Williams, Nina P Jaffe, M David Egan, William J Cavanaugh, and Malcolm Holzman in the preparation of this book. I thank my editors, Nancy Green and Courtney Hirschey, and Norman Hall, the person who introduced me to this arcane profession.

For information about permission to reproduce selections from this book, write to Permissions, W. W. Norton & Company, Inc., 500 Fifth Avenue, New York, NY 10110

For information about special discounts for bulk purchases, please contact W. W. Norton Special Sales at specialsales@wwnorton.com or 800-233-4830

Manufacturing by Everbest Printing Company Ltd.
Book design by Jonathan D. Lippincott
Production manager: Leeann Graham

Library of Congress Cataloging-in-Publication Data

Jaffe, J. Christopher.
   The acoustics of performance halls : spaces for music from Carnegie Hall to the Hollywood Bowl / J. Christopher Jaffe ; foreword by Leo L. Beranek. — 1st ed.
       p.   cm.
   Includes bibliographical references and index.
   ISBN 978-0-393-73255-9 (hardcover)
1. Architectural acoustics. 2. Centers for the performing arts.
3. Music—Acoustics and physics. I. Title. II. Title: Spaces for music from Carnegie Hall to the Hollywood Bowl.
   NA2800.J34 2010
   725'.81—dc22

                                                2009044652

ISBN: 978-0-393-73255-9

W. W. Norton & Company, Inc., 500 Fifth Avenue, New York, N.Y. 10110
www.wwnorton.com

W. W. Norton & Company Ltd., Castle House, 75/76 Wells Street, London W1T 3QT

Frontispiece: Pepsico Recital Hall, Texas Christian University, Fort Worth, Texas. Architect: Hardy, Holzman, Pfeiffer Associates. Acoustics: Jaffe Holden Scarbrough.

CONTENTS

FOREWORD

BY LEO L. BERANEK

Chris Jaffe's *The Acoustics of Performance Halls*—actually music performance halls—is a remarkable presentation of his lifetime of experience as an acoustical consultant to architects, performance administrators, conductors, and building owners all over North America. This book is almost a memoir because Jaffe tells his story in the first person. He shows deep respect for the orchestral sound in famous earlier spaces such as the shoebox halls of Vienna and Boston. He cites the necessary acoustical characteristics in all enclosures where serious music is performed: loudness, intimacy, lateral reflections, envelopment, warmth, clarity, and brilliance. Everywhere in the book, the sound on the performance stage receives major consideration; indeed, one reason for Jaffe's success has been his attention to the needs and whims of performers. An interesting interlude is his description of acoustical memory—how changes in a hall, or the addition of a second hall, frequently is received with disapproval because its sound is compared unfavorably with that of the earlier space that had become well liked.

To meet the challenge of changing times, Jaffe discusses the rise of surround halls, halls in which the room can take on many shapes and where the audience surrounds the performing group. The bellwether was the Berlin Philharmonie, whose resemblance to a shoebox-shaped hall is minimal. Perhaps Jaffe's major contribution to concert hall acoustics has been in the realm of multipurpose halls.

Such halls are common in most cities, where the facilities have to be shared by local theater, orchestra, and opera groups as well as by traveling shows. Also carefully considered by Jaffe are theaters of many shapes with high fly towers or no fly towers. He probably has had more experience than anyone else with music pavilions, particularly those where music is performed in summertime. Here his emphasis on stage acoustics has served him and his clients well. Finally, where natural acoustics cannot be achieved because of a badly shaped hall, Jaffe has experimented extensively with electroacoustic aids.

This personal account of acoustical accomplishments in a wide variety of performance spaces is recommended to architects, managers, owners, musicians, music lovers, and of course all acousticians.

Hanover Square Room, London, England. Late-eighteenth-century recital hall frequently used by Haydn. Architect: Sir John Gallini.

ONE

A DESIGN REVOLUTION

Scientists know that nature is messy and blurry and haphazard and random. The orderliness, the elegant patterns, the neat categories and the mathematical expressions are constructions of scientists. They are not immutable; with new knowledge they change. The overall order of a line of thought comes from paradigms that are often bitterly contested, especially when new ones supersede established ideas. Science then is hardly faith immutable, meaningful laws. Most of it is a search for useful tools and workable processes for manipulating the material world.

—Judith Lorber

The eighteenth and nineteenth centuries were a dynamic and synergistic time in the development of orchestral music. Composers were writing symphonic scores, craftsmen were reinventing string and wind instruments, and musicians were modifying their techniques on these refined and revitalized instruments. Yet all of these exciting developments were taking place in public rooms with an unvarying geometry: narrow, long, and high.

Ironically, these shoebox-shaped rooms were not specifically designed to be optimal concert hall environments. Narrow, high-volume rooms existed for at least 2,500 years before the advent of orchestral music and symphonic ensembles. The late George Izenour, our country's most honored scholar of theater architecture,

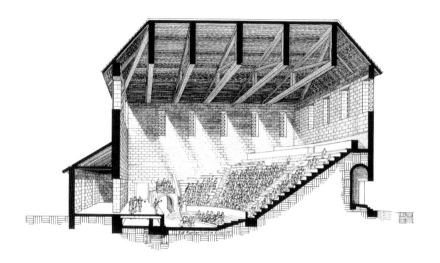

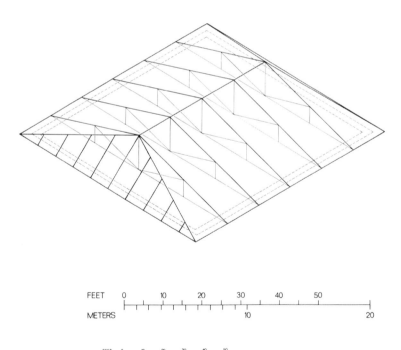

TOP: Odium of Agrippa at Athens, Athens, Greece. Restored plan (after Thompson). Note transverse roof trusses spanning hall. BOTTOM: *Odium of Agrippa at Athens, Athens, Greece. Restored schematic isometric roof structure. Note span is only 55 feet or 17 meters wide.* (From Roofed Theaters of Classical Antiquity *by George C, Izenour. Reproduced with the permission of Rare Books and Manuscripts Special Collections Library, the Pennsylvania State Universities Libraries)*

FEET   0   10   20   30   40   50

METERS   10   20

has noted that from the days of antiquity until the late nineteenth century, no public rooms could be wider than 90 feet (27 meters) without the introduction of support columns. During that period, wood timbers were the only material available for forming long-span trusses. Beyond the length of 90 feet, the trusses would collapse under their own weight.

In his book *Roofed Theaters of Classical Antiquity*, Izenour writes, "From the third century B.C. to the third century A.D., the Hellenistic and Roman architect-builders created an astonishing series of empirical clear-spanned structures that were to remain unsurpassed until the advent of modern structural steel and ferroconcrete technology in the late nineteenth and early twentieth centuries. Principal among these was the structural system that spanned the roofed theatres of this study."

From Athens' Greco-Roman Theater of Athena, built sometime around 424 B.C., to European palace ballrooms and the first public music halls of the eighteenth and nineteenth centuries, all indoor performance rooms were narrow in width. To increase the capacity of these narrow rooms, the obvious solution was to extend the length. Following this method, concertgoers from the sixteenth century through the nineteenth would listen to a performance seated at one end of a long rectangular room with the orchestra at the other end. Other methods for increasing capacity included shallow balconies and parterres (raised areas surrounding the orchestra floor seating).

However, these design elements introduced their own problems. Sight lines from the shallow side balconies to the orchestra platform deteriorate in direct proportion to the balcony's distance from the stage. Beyond 70 feet (22 meters), human features become indistinct. (Try sitting in the last row of the side tier at the back of New York's rectangular Avery Fisher Hall. You have to close the folding seat and sit on the top edge in order to see the musicians onstage). Despite this shortcoming, increasing room length and adding narrow balconies were the only ways to accommodate a large audience at that time.

Not all design hurdles are acoustically based, of course, and those posed by these long and narrow halls were no exception. The air in such a long, narrow room would quickly become stale unless a fresh supply was somehow introduced into the space. In the days before mechanical ventilation systems, the only answer was natural convection. Warm air rises, and if it's allowed to escape through open windows on the side walls near the ceiling, fresh air will flow into the room at a lower level through public entryways. With 500 to 2,000 people in such spaces, considerable height is required in the room to keep a continuous flow of fresh air in the audience seating area and on the orchestra platform. Greco-Roman theaters were built with high roofs and many openings on the side and rear walls of the venue. These design elements were introduced for both ventilation and the day lighting of events.

But most interestingly, the openings that were required for ventilation and day lighting were also essential for the acoustic character of the spaces. With the stone walls, stone seating tiers, and solid wood roofs of most Greek and Roman theaters, the reverberation time (the time it takes sound to disappear in a room) would have been much too long for both speech and small musical ensembles. The large openings in the walls to release the sound, together with an audience seated on the stone tiers to absorb it, brought the room under control for both speech intelligibility and musical clarity. This ventilation scheme was copied in the European concert hall with the location of windows at the top of the side walls of the hall.

Because of the limitations of available structural materials, the desire to accommodate larger audiences, and the need for ventilation, most public concert halls built before 1900 were, as stated earlier, long narrow rooms with high ceilings. Add the bric-a-brac of nineteenth-century architecture and there you are, seated in Vienna's Grosser Musikvereinssaal, which opened in 1870, or the Neues Gewandhaus in Leipzig, built in 1884.

And so it was out of architectural necessity that throughout the eighteenth and nineteenth centuries orchestral music was performed

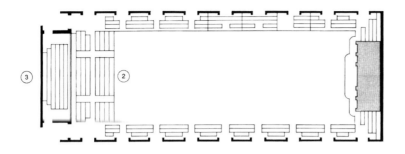

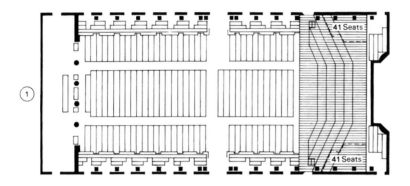

41 Seats

41 Seats

SEATING CAPACITY LARGE STAGE 1598, SMALL STAGE 1680
①   LARGE STAGE 914, SMALL STAGE 1021
②   539
③   120
+ STANDEES

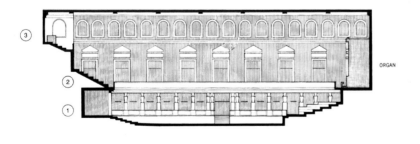

ORGAN

Plan and section drawings of the Grosser Musikvereinssaal, Vienna, Austria. Architect: Theophil Ritter von Hansen.

Grosser Musikvereinssaal, Vienna, Austria, Typical European rectangular concert hall. Architect: Theophil Ritter von Hansen.

in these acoustic environments. Composers such as Haydn, Beethoven, and Mendelssohn were, of course, sensitive to the acoustic ambiance of these spaces, and they fashioned their scores to take advantage of these environments. Performers, in turn, structured their techniques to accommodate these acoustic conditions. The entire musical process—from the composition of a symphonic score to its performance—was based on spaces with similar aural environments. The walls, floors, and ceilings of these spaces reflected sound waves in patterns that laid the foundation for the "traditional" sound of orchestral music, a sound that has shaped the qualitative judgments of most performers and audience members to this day.

For over a century, the Grosser Musikvereinssaal in Vienna has been considered the keeper of the keys, the one hall against which all others must be measured if one is to achieve the "traditional" nineteenth-century orchestral sonic experience. The world-famous conductor Bruno Walter said, "This certainly is the finest hall in the world. It has beauty and power. I had not realized that music could be that beautiful."

Qualitative differences in concert hall sounds can be defined. These differences are based on the relationship of the orchestra's sound—which travels directly to the listener's ear from the instruments themselves—to the sound of reflections generated from the walls, floor, and ceiling of the hall. Some nineteenth-century scientists and musicians may have noted this phenomenon, but they lacked the instrumentation and vocabulary to quantify it.

Today we can conduct comparative tests of listener preferences and match them to measurements of the physical acoustic sound reflections of the room. These reflections create a pattern of energy at each individual seat that acousticians refer to as the hall's "signature." But without the ability to measure reflections in a room, nineteenth-century scientists could not correlate hard data with qualitative subjective judgments. Thus, there was no translation system available to architects who might try to develop alternative geometries with reflection patterns that could replicate the sound being applauded in the long, high, narrow halls. For an architect contracted to design a

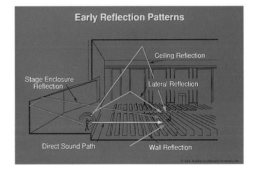

new concert hall during the period from the mid nineteenth century through early twentieth, the safest approach was simply to copy the traditional shoebox geometry that had set the standard for qualitative aural judgments.

Some brave souls did, however, try to break out of this shoebox. Toward the end of the nineteenth century, new and stronger alloys of iron were developed, and engineers began to design buildings made

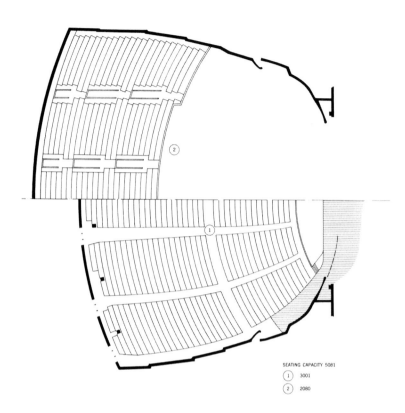

SEATING CAPACITY 5081

(1) 3001

(2) 2080

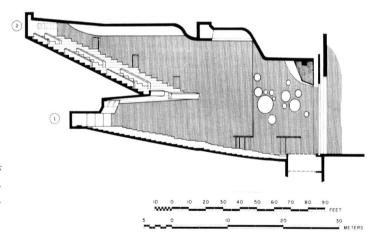

Plans and section drawings
of Orchestra Hall, Chicago.
Architect: Daniel H. Burnham.

10   0   10   20   30   40   50   60   70   80   90
FEET

5   0   10   20   30
METERS

from these materials, which were not only stronger but also lighter than the old wood timbers. With the option of spanning longer distances, architects could change the geometry of concert rooms. It became possible to widen concert halls so that people at the rear of the hall could actually see the musicians. Meanwhile, by introducing modern mechanical ventilation, an architect could lower ceilings, eliminate the windows that were allowing the sounds of the industrial age to disturb listeners, and enable impresarios to schedule concerts from September through May (it wasn't until after World War II and the advent of modern air-conditioning equipment that performance spaces could be used throughout the hot summer months).

In the early twentieth century, before it was possible to collect measurements to correlate with qualitative judgments, some brave architects, such as Daniel H. Burnham and Eliel Saarinen, decided to vary the geometry of their designs, which incorporated new technology. Using steel structures, they built wider halls such as Orchestra Hall in Chicago and Kleinhans Music Hall in Buffalo. The Chicago hall has an average width of 94 feet (29 meters)—as compared with 67 feet (20 meters) at the Grosser Musikvereinssaal. Other wide halls built with steel trusses include the Royal Festival Hall in London and the Konserthus in Gothenburg, Sweden. All four of these halls lack clarity and presence in the orchestra seating area due to their wide widths.

In addition, all of these halls have reduced ceiling heights and are considered low in reverberation times. For example, Orchestra Hall has only 247 cubic feet (7 cubic meters) per person—compared with 315 cubic feet (9 cubic meters) per person at the Grosser Musikvereinssaal. The result is reduced liveness and warmth.

The new dimensions changed the relationship between the direct orchestral sound and the patterns of reflected sound waves. It was a new aural experience that proved unacceptable to many members of the audiences as well as to music critics. The wider halls delayed the arrival of first side-wall reflections to listeners in the center seating areas, resulting in less aural intimacy and definition, and the decreased spatial volume per audience member created a dry, dead acoustic environment. In his book *Concert Halls and Opera Houses*, Leo Beranek reports that "negative criticism of the 1904 Orchestra Hall began the day it opened." Was this bad acoustics? Or was this a different acoustic? Is it possible that some choral works, like Handel's *Messiah*, might actually sound quite good in this space? Might the words of the chorus finally be understood?

At the same time, cities throughout the world were growing in population, and halls with larger seating capacities were in demand. More attendees meant larger halls, which reduced the overall dynamic range of the orchestral performance (what was "soft" in a small hall must become "medium" in a larger one or no one will hear it at all), and in some instances reduced liveness and warmth (as we have seen from Orchestra Hall). Halls with such environments were quickly damned with the judgment "bad acoustics." "Bad" could, of course, be interpreted as unfamiliar. After all, the orchestral music of the preceding two centuries was written to conform to one familiar acoustic environment. The large, rectangular European ballrooms and concert halls of the eighteenth and nineteenth centuries had long been judged appropriate for the music of the Baroque and Classical periods as well as for the Romantic composers of the time, such as Berlioz, Mahler, and Strauss.

Composers of the early twentieth century such as Britten, Holst, and Prokofiev continued to write scores with an ear to the acoustics of the long, high, and narrow performance hall. Many in the musical community, after rejecting the different sounds of the alternative concert hall geometries, insisted that *all* new halls should conform to the standard, traditional design for which music of the last two centuries had been written. Architects and some acousticians, hoping to be praised for their buildings' acoustic quality, continued to copy slavishly the dimensions of the shoebox halls, achieving acoustic environments that were familiar and so labeled successful. Unfortunately, in some instances, they did not truly copy all the characteristics of the nineteenth-century rectangular halls—to their regret.

These designers copied only the *dimensions* of the rough outline of the rooms and neglected to take internal room details and stage acoustic requirements into consideration.

Suddenly, people became aware that even a rectangular shoebox hall must be properly designed to provide reflections that result in the presence, warmth, and clarity that define quality in a performance hall. Those that copied only the outline of the Vienna hall, and neglected to properly copy the interior, failed to meet the expectations of their clients and added to the confusion surrounding symphonic acoustics. If one could not rely on the success of a rectangular hall, what was one to do?

Today most acoustic designers are aware that sound is directly related to the reflecting patterns of sound waves. If you can duplicate the reflection patterns of traditional halls, *regardless of geometry*, you will create the traditional sound. However, at the beginning of the twentieth century, hall owners, orchestras, and designers were reluctant to deviate from what might be called the copycat school of symphony hall design. From within this cloud of misunderstanding, the shoebox emerged as the winning model—although it did not always garner the blue ribbon.

TWO

BREAKING AWAY

Let us proclaim it strongly; the dramatist [composer] will never be able to liberate his vision if he insists upon projecting it in a space rigidly separated from the audience.   —Adolphe Appia

People were enjoying the experience of playing and listening to music long before there were professional architectural acousticians. However, before professional architectural acousticians made their formal debut in concert hall design in the early 1950s, concert hall audiences may have enjoyed the music, but they were unaware of how sound reflections increased the enjoyment of the musical listening experience.

Until the eighteenth century, live concert performances were the province of kings and court. Large-scale public concerts were a relatively new phenomenon. So for most audiences during the nineteenth century and the first half of the twentieth, the opportunity for exposure to this music was in itself a new and sufficiently satisfying experience.

My mother, having studied to become a concert pianist, was typical of the musical cognoscenti of that era. She attended concerts at Carnegie Hall, Town Hall, and the Brooklyn Academy of Music from the late 1920s to the early 1960s. Although chamber music was performed in our living room on many Sunday afternoons, the word "acoustics" was never spoken in our household.

Were my mother and her contemporaries acoustical agnostics? No. Their attention was concentrated, instead, on recently written compositions and on the skills of the performing artists. Listeners may have had an innate sense of certain physical acoustic criteria, such as live versus dry or clear versus muddy, but these aural terms had no measurable counterparts in physical acoustics. There was no scientific vocabulary available to match listeners' musical vocabulary. For the most part, listeners accepted the concert hall environment and took their enjoyment in the interpretation of the music and the technical skills of the artists.

This is not to say that scientists and engineers were not interested in studying architectural acoustic environments as early as the turn of the twentieth century. In 1898, Harvard professor Wallace Clement Sabine, following up on his personal research in architectural acoustics, used his knowledge to help design Boston's Symphony Hall. He developed a pioneering equation that made it possible to calculate a hall's liveness, or reverberation time. The equation states that reverberation time is directly proportional to the room's cubic volume and inversely proportional to the absorptive material in the room. The greater the cubic volume, the more live the space. The more absorption, the deader the space. Here was the early groundwork for a shared vocabulary that would allow musicians and acousticians to finally converse with one another.

Even with this new information, Professor Sabine played it safe and adapted the geometric plan of the Neues Gewandhaus in Leipzig, a new shoebox hall in Germany, as one of the models for Symphony Hall, a room that gained a high acoustic rating among America's best concert halls. Fortunately, he did not replicate the low height of the Neues Gewandhaus, which had a short reverberation time, and instead raised the ceiling, adding nearly .3 second to hall liveness.

With the onset of the twentieth century and the availability of

Symphony Hall, Boston. The premier European shoebox-style concert hall in America. Architect: McKim, Mead & White, Acoustics: Wallace C. Sabine.

steel trusses that could span longer distances, there came another development in architectural design: building materials that could absorb sound in rooms. The longer spans allowed architects to design wider halls with audiences positioned closer to the musicians. New absorptive acoustic building materials, such as special tiles, fiberglass blankets, and mineral fibers, could be placed on the walls and ceilings of a space, thus reducing reverberation and aiding speech clarity in assembly halls, churches, meeting rooms, and radio broadcast and sound recording studios. There were even some acoustical engineers who advocated use of these materials in concert halls to improve musical clarity, despite the fact that too much of these materials would create a dead musical space.

Although Sabine, with the backing of Major Henry Lee Higginson, the founder of the Boston Symphony Orchestra, was able

③

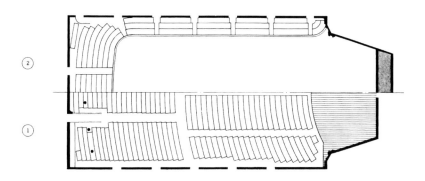

②

①

SEATING CAPACITY 2625

① 1486

② 598

③ 541

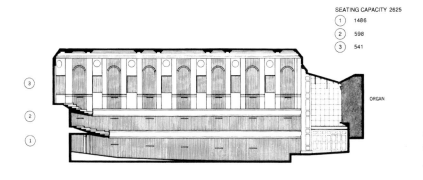

③

②

①

ORGAN

*Plans and section drawings
of Symphony Hall, Boston,
Architect: McKim, Mead &
White. Acoustics: Wallace C
Sabine.*

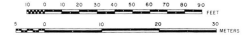

10 0 10 20 30 40 50 60 70 80 90
FEET
5   0   10   20   30
METERS

to modify the original "Greek Amphitheatre" design of architects McKim, Mead & White, other sound professionals were not that fortunate. Physicists and radio engineers were asked for their opinions on the construction of halls and theaters, but they were rarely made an important part of the original design team. Instead, they were called in after the architects had completed their initial concert hall design plans and told to somehow "acousticize" the room. This was the era of the type of arrogant architect fictionalized in *The Fountainhead* who ran roughshod over clients.

We have noted that during the first half of the twentieth century, audiences, for the most part, enjoyed symphony concerts without a true appreciation of the sonic nuances of orchestral performance. This all changed in 1962, the year of the great concert hall acoustic debacle surrounding the opening of Philharmonic Hall at Lincoln Center in New York City.

In the mid-fifties, the power elite of New York City and State decided to raze a slumlike area on Manhattan's Upper West Side to make way for a culture campus comprising buildings for the New York Philharmonic Orchestra, the Metropolitan Opera, the New York City Ballet, the Juilliard School of Music, and a not-yet-named new theater company. The first building to be completed at Lincoln Center was Philharmonic Hall, the new home of the New York Philharmonic. Until this hall opened, the Philharmonic presented all of its concerts at Carnegie Hall, the acoustic crown jewel of American concert halls. Although not a shoebox, Carnegie had sufficient hard wall surfaces to develop the reverberation and warmth associated with the traditional sound. Carnegie might have given acousticians of that time a hint of what geometric changes would be forthcoming in future concert hall designs.

The new Philharmonic Hall was designed as a modified shoebox to mimic the interior of Boston's Symphony Hall, with the addition of overhead reflectors similar to those first used successfully at the Tanglewood Music Pavilion, summer home of the Boston Symphony—but to no avail. The public relations campaign mounted by

Lincoln Center for the new hall was so massive that when it opened in 1962 it could never live up to expectations. Orchestra players complained that they could not hear themselves, and music critics commented that the hall was too bright and the bass response weak. Their dissatisfaction was compounded by the fact that the New York Philharmonic had moved to the new hall at Lincoln Center from the much-beloved Carnegie Hall, a hall with a warm, intimate sound that had been burned into the collective memory of the New York musical community for over sixty years. Musical memory (more properly, perhaps, *sonic* memory) plays an important part in the way individuals perceive an aural experience and their subsequent qualitative judgments.

Philharmonic Hall, Lincoln Center, New York, N.Y. A mid-twentieth-century design based on a European rectangular hall, Architect: Harrison and Abramovitz. Acoustics: Bolt, Beranek & Newman.

Mountains of newspaper coverage were given to this fiasco over a twelve-year period, a good deal of it by Harold Schonberg of the *New York Times*, the most influential classical music critic of the mid-century. With Lincoln Center and the New York Philharmonic struggling to find a voice in the wilderness of musical politics, Mr. Schonberg had a field day writing article after article on the acoustics of the hall as a sort of *All My Children*–type soap opera.

These articles awakened the average listener to fact that there was much more to listening to classical music than the tunes. Mr. Schonberg and others cracked open their old physics textbooks, interviewed dozens of musicians, conductors, and musical scholars, and alerted the public to a slew of new sensory conceptions such as presence, transparency, envelopment, spaciousness, definition, and warmth. The problem was that most of these critics believed that many of these elements were missing from the environment of the new hall, and they didn't hesitate to condemn the facility in article after article. The publicity accompanying the Philharmonic Hall opening and subsequent renovations is the basis for the rumor in New York that Mr. Schonberg invented concert hall acoustics.

The poor critical reception of the new hall's acoustics bolstered the perception that acoustical design was a poorly understood art rather than a true science. After years of tinkering, removing overhead reflectors, relocating balconies, adding side-wall diffusion, lowering the ceiling, and finally building a totally new interior space, the facility reopened in 1976 as Avery Fisher Hall and unfortunately still failed to meet the expectations of musicians and audiences alike.

If a shoebox hall in New York City, one of the world's capitals of music, could fail, what hope was there for the rest of us? However, just as Cowboy Tex always rescued the maiden in distress at the last minute, an acoustic savior appeared in the person of Dr. Leo Beranek, who revolutionized concert and performance hall design by refining the musical acoustic translation system that enabled musicians and acousticians to converse with one another.

A founder of the acoustical consultant firm known as Bolt,

Beranek & Newman, Dr. Beranek had originally been asked to consult on the design for Philharmonic Hall (alas, his many recommendations had been ignored). As part of his preparation for that assignment, Dr. Beranek traveled the globe for several years, attending concerts in dozens of countries and interviewing conductors, musicians, and music critics to obtain their subjective evaluation of the acoustical characteristics of concert halls throughout the world.

At the time of his travels, electronic acoustic instrumentation was sufficiently refined for Beranek to accumulate a wealth of physical acoustic measurements. He then compared this data against the specific subjective observations he had collected. Building on Sabine's work from early in the century, Beranek devised a translation system (see Chapter 3) that finally enabled musicians and architectural acoustic scientists to speak with one another, a virtual

Sala Nezahualcóyotl, Universidad Nacional Autónoma de Mexico, Mexico City. The first surround hall in the Americas. Architects: Orso Nuñez and Arcadio Artis. Acoustics: Jaffe Acoustics.

acoustical Rosetta Stone. Beranek put all of this together in 1962 in a book entitled *Music, Acoustics, and Architecture*, which quickly became a handbook for those of us coming up in the profession. In brief, Beranek asserted that early reflections equaled presence, clarity, and definition, while sufficient reverberation provided liveness and warmth.

Beranek's work segued neatly into the creation of a new profession: the concert hall acoustician. Those of us who applied the new translation system in our design work and appreciated that subjective listening experiences were related to specific characteristics of sound-wave patterns in rooms, not just the geometry, were able to create traditional listening environments without having to copy the architecture or construction materials of nineteenth-century buildings. Acousticians around the world were able to break the mold and design venues such as the Philharmonie in Berlin; the Town Hall Auditorium in Christchurch, New Zealand; the Sala Nezahualcóyotl in Mexico City; the Muziekcentrum Vredenburg, Holland; Boettcher Hall in Denver; and Suntory Hall in Tokyo. They stand as proof that reflecting patterns, not geometry, are the key to reproducing the traditional European symphonic sound environment.

Acousticians were now able to break away from the shoebox geometry and create more intimate environments that matched the traditional sound of the early shoebox halls, those buildings in which the processes of composing and performing symphonies had been born.

THREE

WHERE MUSIC, ACOUSTICS, AND ARCHITECTURE MEET

With oh what cunning skill and patient care

He fashions scientific traps designed

To catch elusive nature unaware

And make her captive to his ruthless mind

With meters, balances and microscope

He tries to pierce the center of her thought.

"By measurements to know"—this is his hope

The Truth in nets and numbers may be caught.

—Paul Sabine

As the last notes of a Mozart violin concerto give way to a rising, pounding tide of applause, we know that the audience is pleased with the sound of the performance. But the acoustician also must satisfy another group of people in the hall: the musicians.

The acoustic success of any concert hall design depends on meeting the subjective responses of these two groups: the performers and the audience, particularly those audience members who might be defined as experienced or trained listeners.

The part of a hall where the performers are located—the stage platform—is known as the "source area." The audience is located in

the "listening area." Since the listening area is fixed in almost every concert hall, it has been possible to correlate subjective judgments of listeners with quantitative measurements of sound reflection in a scientific manner. In the source area, however, musicians playing instruments of different power levels are constantly being repositioned on the stage to accommodate the orchestration of different compositions and conductors' preferences.

I'll begin this description of acoustical design by limiting our discussion to the listening area. We will assume that the balance, blend, and projection of sound in the source area are all perfect.

Thanks to the advent of electronic acoustic instrumentation, we are able to make quantitative measurements of sound reflections in performance halls. However, to construct an acoustically successful hall, we must be able to correlate these *quantitative* physical measurements with the *qualitative* subjective preferences of listeners. In other words, we need to match the qualitative judgments of audience members with quantitative physical measurements of sound in order to create a listener-to-acoustician translation system.

The first comprehensive translation system was developed in the early 1960s by Leo Beranek, the dean of American concert hall acousticians, who, after collecting measurement data and subjective opinions from over sixty halls in twenty nations, published his work, to the benefit of the musical and architectural communities.

In his book, Beranek lists a number of subjective terms used by the musical community to describe the quality of music heard in a concert hall. Among these are: intimacy, presence, liveness, envelopment, warmth, loudness, clarity, definition, and brilliance. Beranek then correlates these terms with a number of physical acoustic measurements such as reverberation times, arrival times of reflections, and loudness, thereby providing an effective translation between the vocabularies of music and acoustics.

It is important to note that this translation system was developed mainly for persons sitting in the listening area of concert halls. There is a separate translation system for the source area of the hall related to the subjective response of musicians located on the performance platform. The design of the source area relies heavily on the skill and the experience of the acoustician in interpreting the musician's reactions. This work might be described as the "art" part of acoustic design.

In developing his translation system, Beranek isolated the subjective attributes that are associated with an outstanding symphonic presentation environment, and then, by relating them specifically to physical measurements of sonic energy, enabled acousticians to design halls that would be favorably received by the entire musical community.

Let's define some of the elements of this subjective vocabulary for the listening area and see how Beranek relates each term to a quantitative scientific vocabulary of acoustics.

INTIMACY AND PRESENCE

In an intimate hall, music sounds as though it is being played in a smaller space. There is an immediate presence to the sound even at the rear of the hall.

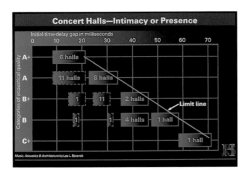

The qualities of intimacy and presence are directly related to the time differential between the arrival of the direct sound of the orchestra emanating from the stage and the receipt of the first reflection from a wall surface or a properly positioned overhead reflector. This time differential is referred to as the "initial time delay gap" (ITDG). An intimate hall has a short initial time delay gap—less than 30 milliseconds. That is why wide halls such as Orchestra Hall in Chicago and the Kleinhans Music Hall are considered deficient in this regard, especially in the center orchestra seating areas, far away from reflecting wall or ceiling surfaces.

LIVENESS AND ENVELOPMENT

A live hall is composed of hard, dense wall, floor, and ceiling surfaces. It allows the sound of the orchestra to persist in a hall for a sufficient amount of time to surround the audience in a 360-degree sonic envelope. Beranek, following Sabine's studies, related liveness or reverberation to the time it takes for a stop chord to die out in a room (also known as decay time)—particularly at the mid-frequency octave bands of 500 to 1,000 cycles per second, now designated as Hertz. (This is the equivalent in the frequency range slightly above middle C to slightly more than two octaves above middle C.)

A live concert hall should have a decay time of 1.8 to 2.1 seconds, balanced with a corresponding

Live Halls	
The mid-frequency reverberation times of seven very good to excellent halls with full audience.	
	Reverberation time in seconds
Grosser Musikvereinssal, Vienna	2.05
Tanglewood Music Shed, Lenox	2.05
Concertgebouw, Amsterdam	2.0
Symphony Hall, Boston	1.8
Teatro Colón, Buenos Aires ca.	1.8
Stadt-Casino, Basel	1.7
Carnegie Hall, New York	1.7

Music, Acoustics & Architecture by Leo L. Beranek

short initial time delay gap. A hall with too long a decay time and a long ITDG will sound muddy and lack clarity.

WARMTH

An outstanding symphonic hall should have a strong, full bass tone, particularly for the lower strings and woodwinds. This subjective response is called warmth, and it is related to the reverberation times at low frequencies (250 Hertz or less; that is, below middle C). In a warm hall, these times will be longer than the reverberation times at the middle frequencies. The ratio of mid-frequency to low-frequency reverberation times is called the bass ratio, and a warm hall will have a bass ratio of 1 or greater.

LOUDNESS

Loudness depends on two elements: the loudness of the direct sound, which is related to the listener's distance from the performer, and the loudness of the reverberant sound, which is related to the hall's size and the absorptive nature of the materials of construction, the seats, and the audience. (Cyril Harris, the acoustician of Orchestra Hall in Minneapolis, placed lockers in the lobby, so audiences during the severe Minnesota winters would not bring their heavy wool and fur coats into the concert hall.)

Seat count can sometimes be the deciding factor in how loud a symphony will sound in a hall, and many owners and users try to push the numbers up. From an acoustician's standpoint, a hall seating 1,800 to 2,200 people provides a good balance between loudness and economic viability. However, one of the best-loved concert halls in the world, the Troy Savings Bank Music Hall in Troy, New York, seats only 1,253 patrons, and the sonic impact on listeners is extraordinary indeed. It isn't often that an owner is

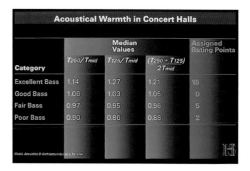

Acoustical Warmth in Concert Halls

Category	T_{250}/T_{mid}	Median Values T_{125}/T_{mid}	$\dfrac{(T_{250}+T_{125})}{2T_{mid}}$	Assigned Rating Points
Excellent Bass	1.14	1.27	1.21	15
Good Bass	1.06	1.03	1.05	9
Fair Bass	0.97	0.95	0.96	5
Poor Bass	0.90	0.86	0.88	2

Music, Acoustics & Architecture by Leo L. Beranek

willing to bear the expense of building a large-volume hall with a limited audience capacity. The Troy Hall has all the requisite criteria for an excellent symphonic environment plus a dynamic range not found in larger halls.

CLARITY AND DEFINITION

A hall with clarity and definition is self-explanatory. It will enable listeners to hear the complex strands of Bach and Mozart compositions as well as the inner voices of thickly scored symphonic passages by later composers. Although some listeners may consider this a separate entity, it's closely related to presence and intimacy and depends on the early arrival time of first reflections.

BRILLIANCE

Brilliance is related, among other variables, to the reverberation times at high frequencies compared to those at low frequencies. Brilliance has been defined as an integration of other qualities: liveness at high frequencies, clarity, and intimacy. One must be careful, however, that the sound of the treble doesn't predominate over the bass. When this occurs, a hall's sound can become too bright and sharp, as opposed to warm and intimate.

When reviewing the above criteria, you will note that reverberation times, the initial time delay gap, and the bass ratio are the three critical measurements that can correlate to a listener's subjective evaluation of a symphonic environment. These three criteria together with loudness form the basis of all key objective acoustic criteria related to concert hall design.

Starting with Beranek's three basic criteria, I and my colleagues at Jaffe Acoustics

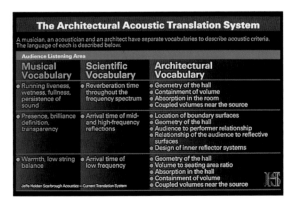

The Architectural Acoustic Translation System

A musician, an acoustician and an architect have separate vocabularies to describe acoustic criteria. The language of each is described below.

Audience Listening Area

Musical Vocabulary	Scientific Vocabulary	Architectural Vocabulary
● Running liveness, wetness, fullness, persistence of sound	● Reverberation time throughout the frequency spectrum	● Geometry of the hall ● Containment of volume ● Absorption in the room ● Coupled volumes near the source
● Presence, brilliance definition, transparency	● Arrival time of mid- and high-frequency reflections	● Location of boundary surfaces ● Geometry of the hall ● Audience to performer relationship ● Relationship of the audience to reflective surfaces ● Design of inner reflector systems
● Warmth, low string balance	● Arrival time of low frequency	● Geometry of the hall ● Volume to seating area ratio ● Absorption in the hall ● Containment of volume ● Coupled volumes near the source

Jaffe Holden Scarbrough Acoustics – Current Translation System expanded the translation system for the listening area by developing a vocabulary for the architect, who has the responsibility of integrating our acoustic requirements with his or her vision of the space. First, using the Beranek information, we converted the vocabulary of the musician to that of the physical scientist. Then we translated the scientific vocabulary into one of architectural design.

When an audience member speaks subjectively of a hall's intimacy, the subjective attribute can be described by specific physical phenomena of sound waves moving in space. Understanding this relationship lets the acoustician provide the architect with data to help him or her decide on the width of a hall and the location of inner terrace walls and overhead sound reflectors—decisions that enable the architect to design a space with an intimate environment.

The table shows our double translation system for the listening area, with musical and architectural terminologies related to the acoustic "scientific" vocabulary. The many different descriptors of music and architecture are correlated to just three acoustical terms— i.e., initial time delay gap, reverberation time, and bass ratio—thus streamlining both communication and design.

Does the system really work? Can you base a concert hall's design on just three acoustical criteria? Jaffe Acoustics has used these three acoustical descriptors to design symphonic facilities of very different architectural styles. All of these facilities incorporated the correlations between the reflections of sound in the hall and listener preferences. And all were extremely well received by audiences, performers, and the music press.

So, with just three physical criteria in hand, we can embark on the acoustical design of a hall's listening area. Here are our four design goals:

1. First we need to *strike the proper balance between liveness and clarity*. These attributes, as we've seen, are related to the hall's reverberation time and initial time delay gap.
2. When striking a balance between liveness and clarity, we

must make sure that *intimacy, definition, and transparency are all developed* by selecting the proper initial time delay gap in all of the seating locations.

3. We want the hall to *provide a warm tone for the lower string instruments*—a criterion related to the bass ratio. That means furnishing plenty of the familiar, bass-rich low frequencies that are the hallmark of traditional concert hall sounds.

4. We must *avoid any acoustical faults*—such as obstructions, hard concave surfaces or other echo-producing surfaces—that might interfere with the audience's reception of unsullied direct and reflected sound fields.

Implementing the three criteria to achieve these four goals is the responsibility of the acoustical consultant, and the success of the project depends on his or her skill in integrating the criteria with the design requirements of all the other professionals working on the project—as well as with the aspirations of the owners and users of the facility.

With a clear understanding of listening area acoustics, we can now look at the acoustics of the stage platform, the location of the source of orchestral music in a hall.

FOUR

THE ORCHESTRA PLATFORM—
THE LAST FRONTIER

The final test of acoustics is what the audience hears, but no one should under-
estimate how the singer perceives acoustics while performing.

—Placido Domingo

Over the last thirty years, acoustical researchers have carefully explored the relationship between concert hall listening quality and physical acoustic measurements. This work has been quite successful, because both the measurements and the judgments were made from specific seats in the auditorium in relation to the direct orchestral sound and all room reflections. The only variable that might affect liveness and warmth would be the size of the audience. Audience absorption is a major factor in the Sabine equation calculation.

But the emphasis of this research was on the quality of sound in the *listening* area, and not enough attention was paid to the character and quality of sound on the orchestral stage platform, or *source* area. Why did this occur?

1. Traditional concert halls are one-room affairs without features like prosceniums (the arch in a multiuse theater that frames the stage and separates it from the audito-

rium). So, conventionally, the orchestra platform was not considered a separate environment.

2. Until recently, it wasn't considered terribly important for musicians to hear themselves and other members of the ensemble in terms of on-time entrances and maintaining pitch. In fact, the musicians' ability to hear one another greatly improves sound quality in a room, but many concert hall designers did not give that concept sufficient weight.

Many orchestra managements belittled the journeyman musician, and very little consideration was given to his or her comfort level on stage, aural or otherwise (ask any orchestra musician you know). In two instances, one in Monterrey, Mexico, and the other in Istanbul, Turkey, hall management positioned overhead ceiling reflectors in relation to concert lighting so the musicians had to choose between hearing themselves or reading their music (reading their music won the day).

Next to on-stage hearing, orchestral sectional balance is one of the most important factors in the source area. The higher-powered brass and percussion instruments are located at the rear of the orchestra platform, with the woodwinds and strings placed forward of these sections. This is done to provide the conductor with a reasonable balance between the power levels of the direct sound of the various sections. However, in many halls, the reinforcement given to the brass and percussion sections of the orchestra due to reflections from the rear wall of the hall can overwhelm the lower-powered string and woodwind instruments located 25 to 40 feet away from this surface. This is especially true of string instruments in the lower sonic registers (viola, cello, and double bass), since humans are not as aurally sensitive to low tones as they are to higher ones. Audience members, whose aural perception is strongly related to reflected sound energy, would be more aware of these imbalances than the conductor, who is positioned just a few feet away from the strings and woodwinds.

In terms of the single-purpose European concert hall, orchestral balance was sometimes improved by placing a pipe organ or choral seating behind the orchestra platform. The absorptive characteristics of the thin wood organ cabinets as well as those of seat cushions provided some relief. However, these solutions were not readily available for the American-style multiuse hall with a full stage loft behind the proscenium arch.

My early work with orchestras revealed that physical changes in the source area had a tremendous impact on the quality of sound emanating from the stage. These changes related to varying the location of orchestral sections on the stage, repositioning movable overhead reflectors (panels of fiberglass, wood, or other materials suspended over the orchestra platform), and introducing risers for certain sections of the orchestra. (Risers are platforms for performers that raise the musicians at the back of the orchestra to a level higher than those in front.)

Since it is extremely expensive to schedule sufficient rehearsal time to experiment with the positioning of reflectors and risers when dealing with the contract requirements of fully professional orchestras, ideal formats are hard to realize. Musicians' contracts limit the amount of time they are permitted to rehearse and perform, and conductors cherish every available minute working on the musical program. Almost all my tuning work was done during regularly scheduled performance rehearsals, and major changes had to be made during breaks in the schedule.

Obtaining meaningful opinions from musicians related to physical changes made on or near the performance platform is not easy. Traditionally, such opinions have been gathered in situ. Whether acousticians are working in multipurpose halls with reflectors suspended from existing rigging or in one-room concert halls where the rigging has to be temporarily installed to accommodate overhead physical reflectors or diffusers, judgments are made primarily by the acousticians and administrative personnel in the listening area. The musicians on stage, participating in a working rehearsal, have difficulty providing definitive opinions on the various setups. They are given questionnaires and asked to make instant qualitative judgments *while* physical changes are made on and around the orchestra platform. This is an extremely unsatisfactory method of obtaining meaningful subjective information, since the musicians, concentrating on the score and the conductor's baton, are distracted and the tabulated results of the questionnaires are erratic and inconsistent. In some cases, half the orchestra doesn't even bother to fill out the forms.

More recently, technological advances in binaural recording techniques that place microphones in replicas of human heads have enabled acousticians to obtain more accurate subjective data from musicians during working rehearsals. These systems record in the same way human beings hear, and when the recordings are played back at a later time, musicians can listen again without the distraction of playing at the same time. The musicians can then give accurate qualitative opinions about the source area's key acoustic characteristics as physical changes are made on stage. For example: We can install microphones in the two ears of a "dummy head"—a replica of a human head and torso—and binaurally record small sections of an orchestral score as physical changes are made in and around the stage platform.

Nina Jaffe with "Fritz," the Aachen dummy head tuning the renovated Jackie Gleason Performing Arts Center, Miami Beach, Florida. Architect: Sasaki Associates. Acoustics: Jaffe Acoustics.

The orchestra repeats these segments after each change is completed. These changes might include repositioning reflector panels and adding or removing stage risers and/or diffuser panels.

Although we can make quantitative measurements of various experimental physical setups, it would not do us much good, since different compositions are scored for a constantly changing number of musicians positioned at different locations on the stage platform and performing on a variety of different instruments. The subjective responses of musicians to dummy head recordings are a better indicator of the acoustic environment on the stage platform than in situ questionnaires or measurements of physical acoustic reflective energy.

Since dummy head recordings provide us with qualitative information that is much more definitive than orchestra surveys, our next step is to correlate the qualitative subjective preferences of listeners—in this case, the orchestra members—with the physical changes made to the stage platform and surfaces surrounding this area of the hall. A typical example of such an evaluation rehearsal was conducted several years ago at Avery Fisher Hall in Lincoln Center after musicians complained of poor onstage hearing. The surfaces surrounding the stage platform in the hall are composed of dense wood paneling and shaped in hornlike configurations. The wall and ceiling surfaces are slightly articulated and there are no inner reflector systems suspended from the ceiling.

Although the conductor of the orchestra was quoted as saying that the listening area of the hall is "very good," he was concerned that "the sound between musicians is not at the highest level we should expect." For this reason, the orchestra commissioned me to recommend modifications of the stage platform that would improve onstage hearing and orchestral balance. The variable physical elements included overhead reflectors, diffuser panels surrounding the performance platform, orchestra risers, and a stage extension.

The testing process itself was conceived around the use of an in situ orchestra survey and a subsequent evaluation of recordings made by the Aachen Head, the technically advanced binaural measurement microphone system that simulates the human hearing process. For the tests, the conductor selected (and the acoustical consultants approved) works and segments for the orchestra to play.

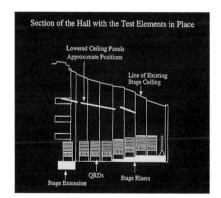

Section of the Hall with the Test Elements in Place

Lowered Ceiling Panels Approximate Positions

Line of Existing Stage Ceiling

Stage Extension   QRDs   Stage Risers

We collected responses via a survey of the musicians, while at the same time we took binaural recordings of specific segments of music during two special acoustic test rehearsals. Recordings were made from three locations on stage and one seat in the house. The musicians performed under the following experimental conditions:

Test	Stage Configuration
A	Ceilings and diffusers in place, stage extension in use
B	Ceilings and diffusers in place, stage extension not in use
C	Ceilings in place, stage extension not in use
D	Ceilings in place, stage extension in use
E	Existing stage, stage extension not in use
F	Existing stage with string risers in place, stage extension not in use
G	Existing stage with diffusers and string risers in place, stage extension not in use

Acoustical consultants developed the orchestra questionnaire used for both tests. The orchestra reviewed the proposed survey and offered suggestions for refinements, some of which were incorporated into the final form of the questionnaire. Musicians responded to six criteria for each test after each modification was completed. The criteria and their descriptions were as follows:

1. Self-Hearing—How well can you hear yourself?
2. Orchestra Hearing—How well can you hear the rest of the orchestra?
3. Volume Level—How do you find the overall level of sound on stage?
4. Harshness/Smoothness—How is the sound quality? Harsh and imprecise, or smooth and clearly defined?
5. Warmth, or Bass Response—Is the orchestra sound warm

and rich—that is, can you hear the bass line easily?

6. Overall Rating—Your overall score for this stage setup.

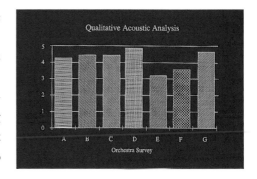

Musicians were asked to rate each of the criteria on a scale of 1 to 9, with 1 always representing the poorest rating and 9 always representing the best score, and on the survey was provided a space to record their comments.

As the results clearly indicate, the musicians consistently expressed a preference for the stage acoustics *after* the introduction of the lowered ceiling and/or the diffusion. We see this clearly in the sharp negative ratings for Tests E and F (existing stage conditions) versus the ratings for situations including the overhead ceilings and the diffuser panels, Tests A, B, C, D, and G. However, it was impossible to evaluate the changes made during tests A, B, C, D, and G because the musician survey results did not indicate any statistical preferences for these changes.

In order to evaluate conditions A, B, C, D, and G and determine which of these formats were best received by the musicians, the consultants prepared a series of binaural listening tests using material recorded during the two days of testing in the hall.

The results of the blind jury testing illustrate the preferences of the orchestra musicians much more clearly than the results of the orchestra surveys. While there were differences of opinion for different music segments or for different listening positions, the overall trends that emerge from the tests indicate an unambiguous preference for the Test B condition (ceiling and diffusers in place, stage extension not in use).

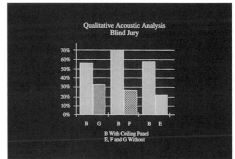

The figures shown are the averages derived from all of the listening locations and music segments tested. Test B is always preferred by a decisive

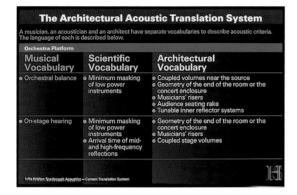

The Architectural Acoustic Translation System

A musician, an acoustician and an architect have separate vocabularies to describe acoustic criteria. The language of each is described below.

Orchestra Platform

Musical Vocabulary	Scientific Vocabulary	Architectural Vocabulary
● Orchestral balance	● Minimum masking of low power instruments	● Coupled volumes near the source ● Geometry of the end of the room or the concert enclosure ● Musicians' risers ● Audience seating rake ● Tunable inner reflector systems
● On-stage hearing	● Minimum masking of low power instruments ● Arrival time of mid- and high-frequency reflections	● Geometry of the end of the room or the concert enclosure ● Musicians' risers ● Coupled stage volumes

Artin Hriŝten Scarbrough Acoustics — Current Translation System

margin.

This series of measurements, recordings, surveys, and jury sessions revealed great promise for the use of binaural techniques in subjective acoustical evaluations on the orchestra platform. Binaural recording heads and sophisticated binaural analysis systems offer acoustical researchers a new way to examine acoustical phenomena and to relate these to subjective impressions.

Unlike our qualitative *listening* area descriptors, which can be correlated to a vocabulary of scientific quantitative measurements, qualitative *source* area descriptors are best related to architectural vocabularies, necessitating a different translation system for the source area to guide us in concert hall design.

Based on years of experience tuning orchestra stages and having much of this information confirmed through evaluation rehearsals, I codified some more or less universal preferences of musicians to assist architects in designing the stage area of a concert hall. The goal is twofold: to inform architectural decisions in designing the stage area of a concert hall, and to assist concert managers in realizing the best possible sound. On the managers' wish list:

1. Balance the acoustical energy output of the various sections of the orchestra.
Reduce a portion of the energy of the brass and percussion instruments at the back wall of the stage or concert shell, so that these sections do not overpower the lower-energy strings and woodwinds further downstage. This can be accomplished by adding small amounts of absorptive or diffusing material on the rear wall, placing operable grill openings in the rear wall, or opening up a larger space between the last ceiling panel of a concert shell and the rear wall.

To obtain a better balance between the woodwinds and the

strings and brass, use platform risers for the woodwind players, who are positioned directly behind the second violins and the violas. The brass, horns, and timpani can be on risers of similar height or slightly higher for sight-line purposes.

To increase the sound levels of cellos and double basses, make sure that the pegs of their instruments are in direct contact with the wooden floor of the stage. This will transfer energy to the stage floor, setting it in vibration to augment the sound of these instruments. Some cellos and bass players like to affix a rubber piece to the peg of their instrument to give it more stability. Take these pieces off the instruments as soon as you observe that they are being used.

In some instances it might be advisable to position the bass players on tuned riser platforms. Each player is placed on an individual boxed riser that is tuned to a pitch close to that of the lowest string of the instrument. Holes are cut into the side of the riser to allow sound energy to enter the room, and absorptive material is placed inside the box to spread the effect over a wide range of frequencies and prevent the tuned riser from producing a single pitch.

2. Blend the individual instruments into a single musical entity.
Make sure that the side and rear surfaces of the performance platform are in close proximity to the instrumentalists. For instance, in a surround hall, where the walls of the room are 20 or more feet away from the stage, it is essential to build walls about 10 feet high surrounding the players in order to adequately blend the orchestral sound. The enclosures made by these walls are sometimes referred to as bear pits.

3. Distribute the balanced and blended sound throughout the listening area.
In a one-room concert hall, there usually is nothing to interfere with the balanced and blended sound between the source and listening areas. In a multipurpose hall with the orchestra seated behind the

proscenium arch, an acoustic enclosure or shell must be designed to project the sound through the arch opening. The side walls of this shell must be angled to project the sound outward and the ceiling of the shell must be shaped to do the same thing.

4. Enable the musicians to hear themselves and other sections of the orchestra.
All of the design elements listed under items 1, 2, and 3 will assist the musicians in hearing themselves and others: e.g., close proximity to side and rear reflectors, stage risers, tuned bass risers, and, in the case of the multipurpose hall, overhead ceilings or reflectors.

5. Develop a warm environment on stage.
If all the architectural surfaces are designed to the acousticians' specifications, with the acoustic elements positioned properly, and the room still lacks musical warmth, the volume of the hall is probably low because of the absorption characteristics of the space.

When the volume of a hall is too low because of the absorption factor, the mid-range and high frequencies are more prevalent, the bass ratio is out of balance (lower than 1), and the hall will not provide a warm environment. Under these circumstances, it may be necessary to add volume in the vicinity of the orchestra platform to reinforce bass resonance. This is discussed in more detail in the case studies of the Kennedy Center Concert Hall in Washington, D.C., Severance Hall in Cleveland, and Bass Hall in Fort Worth.

Although I have developed separate translation systems for the listening and the source areas, sound energy does travel between these locations—the reverberant characteristic of the listening area will affect on-stage hearing and the two areas must be satisfactorily blended. Many architectural acoustic texts use single-figure average specifications as guides in room acoustic design. However, most practicing acousticians would agree that the acoustic environment of a concert hall varies from the source to the listening area (particularly in terms of the relationship between the direct and reverberant

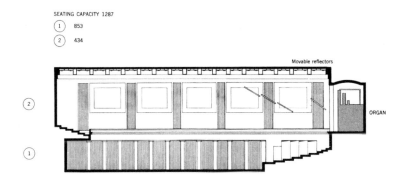

SEATING CAPACITY 1287
① 853
② 434

Movable reflectors

ORGAN

Section of the Herkulessaal, Munich. Overhead reflectors in a European rectangular hall. Architect: Rudolf Esterer. Acoustics: E. Meyer and R. Thiele.

sound fields), and a key factor in the success of a hall is the proper relationship of sound energy in these locations. How we develop the relationship between the two sets of acoustic conditions determines the hall's overall environment for musical presentations and may be considered the "art" portion of the acoustician's work. This is where experienced, acoustically trained ears come into play.

When we study a single-space concert hall in the traditional shoe-box style—like Boston's Symphony Hall or the Musikvereins-saal—we discover that our design goals for the source area may have already been met by the floor, wall, and ceiling designs of the hall near the stage. In other words, the envelope of the room itself provides the acoustics that match our required criteria.

But this is not always the case. In some single-space concert halls, the envelope of the stage area *doesn't* provide the necessary source area acoustic criteria. Symphony halls in Stockholm, Berlin, Munich, and Rotterdam have improved their sound quality onstage by adding and sometimes subtracting architectural elements in these areas using suspended panel reflectors, absorptive material, and diffusers. The boundary surfaces surrounding the stage platform in a single-purpose concert hall do not always meet required source area criteria.

Now that we understand the criteria for the audience seating area and the stage platform of a concert hall, let's actually design both a shoebox and a surround-style single-purpose concert hall.

FIVE

DESIGNING THE "SHOEBOX" CONCERT HALL

Scientists seek explanations of phenomena through observable events. These explanations are good to the extent that they jibe with past observations and are able to predict future events. —Chance Reschke

The design of a concert hall is a team effort. The key players are the owner, the users, the acoustician, the architect, the theater consultant, and the project manager. The supporting cast will include a structural engineer, a mechanical engineer, an electrical engineer, a landscape architect, a cost consultant, and a management consultant. I subscribe to the theory that the best facilities are built when the team is working with knowledgeable owners and users who have a clear vision of the program uses of the hall.

Let's say that the reader is the acoustician and follow the process through his or her eyes. The first step is to determine that the program developed by the owner, possibly with the assistance of a feasibility study, is the final version on which the design team will base its work. The owner must formally sign off on this document.

In this particular instance, the clients have decided that they desire a one-room concert hall that will handle the full range of classical ensembles from soloists and quartets to hundred-piece symphony orchestras with chorus. A pipe organ must be incorporated in the design, and the hall must accommodate performances of jazz, world music, and contemporary electronic compositions. In addition, they would like to stage concert versions of musical comedy, modern dance recitals, and a variety of amplified popular music presentations.

The team's first response might be, why don't these characters ask us to design a multiuse hall? On second thought, they realize that 90 percent of the program is music-related and that none of the theater and dance programs suggested require a stage house (a large towerlike space over the stage where scenery is stored between acts) or large wing spaces. A major acoustic concern still exists. Many of these music performances will require different acoustic environments for successful presentations, and acousticians must be cognizant of the fact that even in a one-room symphonic concert hall, they will have to provide some variable acoustic elements as well as a sound system for amplified programs. This holds true for major concert halls as well as for university facilities. Major concert halls like Carnegie Hall and Avery Fisher Hall need every penny they can earn from off-symphony nights. Both are terrible spaces for amplified popular events. Today's new concert halls must have some acoustic modification treatments to enable them to book non-musical events and amplified music. (Once, an international squash tournament was held in Boston's Symphony Hall. A large number of the orchestra seats were removed, a clear plastic box was erected in the hall in a thrustlike configuration, and the spectators watched the match from three sides.)

Two other items must be resolved by the client, with input from the team, before we start the design process. The first is related to the seating capacity of the hall. Some programs may draw only 1,000 people, and others may draw as many as 5,000 patrons. Owners may be blinkered by monetary considerations. However, the key isn't the number of seats that are in your hall, but the number of seats that you can sell at a price that is remunerative and affordable. In this instance, for the design of a dedicated symphony hall, the acoustician must

Abravanel Symphony Hall, Salt Lake City, Utah. Another modern hall design based on a European rectangular hall. Architect: Fowler, Ferguson, Kingston, Ruben. Acoustics: Cyril M. Harris.

insist on keeping the seat count down to approximately 2,200 people in order not to comprise hall loudness. The more absorptive people in a hall, the more air volume needed to maintain the proper reverberation time. Greater air volume will reduce overall hall loudness.

The second question is related to the style of the hall. Does your client want an end stage or a surround hall? This is a tricky question, since both can deliver the traditional European sound. The end stage hall is more formal and more conservative, while the surround hall is more egalitarian and more contemporary. The answer to this question must come from the client and in many ways is related more to the lifestyle of the community and the sentiments of the conductor and the musicians than to any acoustic issues. When relying on a conductor's opinion, we must remember that, in today's symphonic world, conductors do not stay on board as long as some of the maestros of old, such as Arturo Toscanini, Leopold Stokowski, and George Szell. Szell stayed with the Cleveland Orchestra for twenty-four years, and Stokowski conducted the Philadelphia Orchestra for twenty-eight years. Compare these with the shorter tenures of Pierre Boulez at the New York Philharmonic or Riccardo Muti in Philadelphia. Therefore, the opinions of the musicians and other members of the local musical community should carry a little more weight.

Now we are ready to begin to design the hall. The acoustician must start the design process and provide the architect and the rest of the team with whatever criteria are required to make the hall work for all these events.

The acoustician will start by realizing that this is first and foremost a classical music hall, and that well-received halls such as Carnegie Hall, the Troy Savings Bank Music Hall in Troy, New York, and the recently renovated Kennedy Center Concert Hall present a wide assortment of classical ensembles as well as amplified popular music in the acoustical environment of the traditional European concert hall. Therefore, let's set the basic criteria for our hall on these models and determine how we might modify the environment for good speech intelligibility and amplified music programs as we go along.

The Auditorium in the Christchurch Town Hall for Performing Arts, New Zealand. One of the earliest surround concert halls. Architect: Warren & Mahoney. Acoustics: A. H. Marshall.

We'll start on the assumption that the client wants a rectangular end stage hall and work through the design process. Bear in mind that end stage halls come in three different geometric shapes: rectangular, fan, or reverse fan. Since we have learned that it is the reflecting patterns that must be duplicated to achieve the traditional European sound, these options should be reviewed with the client and the architect in terms of architectural style. The fan and reverse fan halls will require forestage reflector systems over a portion of the audience area that may or may not be in line with the client's or the architect's vision of the space. (Let's hope that the client selected an architect who was representative of the client's lifestyle and design preferences. It's too early for a fight.) For this rectangular hall, we'll proceed with shoebox geometry.

As discussed, in order to duplicate the sound of a traditional European hall, we must set criteria for reflecting patterns that will accomplish this objective and then translate these criteria in terms that will enable the architect to begin designing the physical room. Since it is the geometry of the traditional end stage hall that created the traditional sound, providing instructions for the architect should not be too difficult.

LISTENING AREA ACOUSTIC CRITERIA

We have determined that this hall is primarily a classical music facility and that as such it must limit its seating capacity to 2,200 people. Anything larger will reduce loudness, require enormous volume to compensate for audience absorption, destroy sight lines at the rear of side balconies, and distance many members of the audience from the performers on stage.

The hall must be narrow, with a width that does not exceed 90 feet wall-to-wall, in order to provide the proper initial time delay gap of less than 20 to 30 milliseconds. (As stated before, the early reflections from the walls of the narrow hall will provide clarity, intimacy, transparency, and presence.)

In addition, the ratio between the volume of the hall and the seating capacity (the audience being the source of most of the absorption in a concert hall) should result in a reverberation time at mid frequency of 1.8 to 2.1 seconds. The formula for calculating reverberation time is given as

RT = 0.5 × volume of hall ÷ sum of all the absorption in the hall

In a hall with an audience capacity of 2,000 people, we would require the architect to provide a volume of 700,000 cubic feet (19,821 cubic meters) in order to achieve a 2.0-second reverberation time (the amount necessary to provide liveness and envelopment for the audience).

Side balconies must be limited to two rows to reduce the overhang factor and maintain sight lines from the rear side balcony seats. The rear balcony should be limited to three or four rows to reduce the overhang factor for those members of the audience seated at the rear of the main floor. If part of the rear balcony is positioned over a portion of the lobby, it is possible to add some additional rows.

The construction materials for the walls and ceiling of the hall should be massive and stiff to contain low-frequency energy in the hall. (This will provide the proper ratio of mid- to low-frequency reverberation needed for warmth.)

The floor of the audience area should be made of wood and rigidly connected to the wooden stage floor so as to gain additional low-frequency structural vibration that will further enhance warmth.

SOURCE AREA ACOUSTIC CRITERIA

A contemporary symphonic stage should be approximately 2,400 square feet (223 square meters) to accommodate 100 musicians and a standing chorus of 150 to 200 members. The downstage width should be 60 feet (19 meters) and the upstage width 45 feet (14 meters). The depth of the stage should be at least 40 feet (12 meters). The stage width can be adjusted accordingly to obtain an optimum relationship between the widths of the hall, any side seating locations (parterres), and the stage. The parterre can wrap around the stage and can accommodate choruses as required. When the chorus is not performing, these seats can be sold to the public.

The pipe organ can be set behind the choral seating area at a level just above the parterre and be played from an electronic console

THE ACOUSTICS OF PERFORMANCE HALLS

onstage. The organ should be designed as a symphonic instrument with plenty of power.

The first balcony should wrap around the stage and should butt against the organ casing at either end. The second balcony should do the same. However, the section of the second balcony that wraps around the stage should be a tech balcony and not incorporate any audience seating. This will enable the acoustician to place some reflectors over the stage, if required, and not block sound and sight lines to those sitting in these locations. (The walls of the parterre and the right angle that is made between the hall walls and the undersides of the two balconies will provide a great deal of early reflections to members of the orchestra, thus enabling them to hear themselves and one another. In addition, these surfaces will assist in blending the orchestral sound into a unified whole).

Since the volume above the orchestra and that above the audience is contiguous, the reverberation times in both locations will be similar and the performers will enjoy a strong aural return from the room. (This means that vocalists will not have to push or strain their voices and instrumentalists will not have to force their tones.)

One question that arises at this point: will those musicians at the center of the stage receive as much benefit from early side reflections coming from the parterres and the upper wall angles as those at the edges of the ensemble? In my experience, the answer is no, and some overhead reflectors would be in order. The problem is, we don't want these reflectors to cut off the sound and the spectacular view of the organ when they are in position.

To handle the sight-line problem, these reflectors ideally would be made of glass or clear acrylic. Acoustically, they don't have to provide complete overhead coverage for the entire ensemble, since we are still obtaining a lot of early reflections from the walls, the fronts of the parterre, and the organ casings at the rear of the stage platform. In terms of organ sound, these reflectors can be raised by electromechanical means for the few times an organ is needed for symphonic compositions and when solo organ recitals are scheduled.

OVERALL ACOUSTIC DESIGN DIRECTION

How can we keep sound from the lobbies and backstage locations from entering the hall? By isolating the hall from these areas with sound locks in the form of corridors and air locks between two sets of doors. If one cannot find the space for sound locks, special sound-rated door constructions must be specified for these locations.

What techniques will we use to keep mechanical-system noise to the low levels required for concert performances? This question must be resolved with the coordinated efforts of the mechanical and

Winspear Hall, University of North Texas, Denton, Texas. A contemporary design of a rectangular hall. Architect: Hardy Holzman Pfeiffer Associates. Acoustics: Jaffe Holden Scarbrough.

structural engineers as well as with the architect. Huge ducts are required to reduce the sound levels of the fans that provide cool as well as fresh air to the hall. These large ducts also reduce air turbulence noise in the system as well. The architect and structural engineer have to consider how these elements can be placed among the steel trusses or concrete beams that will support the structure, and coordination between all the team members in regard to integrating all these elements is essential. The team must also provide spaces for vertical and/or horizontal duct chases, or accessways, that will allow the ducts from the mechanical room to be distributed throughout the building.

The acoustician will take the lead in regard to sound control by setting a noise criteria level (NC level) for an air-handling system in the hall as well as for all other sound-critical spaces in the building (e.g., lobby, stage house, performance platform, rehearsal room, warm-up rooms, dressing rooms, green room, etc.). In addition, the acoustician will furnish the mechanical engineer with basic criteria for air velocity, duct silencers, and other elements to enable him or her to design the systems. Separate air-handling systems will be developed for the hall, stage, lobby, and backstage to avoid cross talk from one room system to another. As the mechanical system is designed, the acoustician will review the mechanical engineers' work to make sure that his calculations meet the desired noise criteria set for all the spaces. A critical item to remember is that backstage duct runs must travel through corridors, and trunk lines off these main ducts must be provided to supply each room.

If the hall is being built near an airport, an interstate highway, or a subway line, the acoustician may have to call on acoustical vibration specialists to determine how to isolate the hall from noise related to these sources. Isolating subway noise at Zankel Hall and Alice Tully Hall in New York City required the assistance of specialists in this field.

So that is the start. Where do our acoustician and team go from here? To a back-and-forth design process through schematic design,

design development, and even construction documentation. Any number of hurdles are likely to pop up: The wonderful low-noise fan used on the last project is no longer manufactured, and the new fan is noisier. . . . One will have to add sound traps, longer duct runs, or sound plenum chambers (pressurized absorbtive spaces between the end of the duct runs and the hall itself) to reach the original noise criteria specified for the hall. The architect wants a curved rear wall that will focus sound. . . . the acoustician will have to develop a diffusion surface that will break up the sound waves and eliminate echoes.

These are just brief samples of the give-and-take of acoustic design in a building. At some point, the cost consultant will inform the team that they are over budget and the whole group will point fingers at the acoustician, who has specified 70-foot-high ceilings and custom seats with low absorption characteristics. This is a good time to put on your Tony Soprano dark glasses, clench your teeth, and hold the line. Do we really need all that Italian marble on the lobby floor?

VARIABLE ACOUSTIC DESIGN ELEMENTS

At some point during the schematic design phase, the acoustician will have to develop a method for varying the acoustic environment of the space so that the client can successfully present amplified programs that require reduced reverberation times and increased speech intelligibility. This can be accomplished in a variety of ways, and here again we must develop separate approaches for the listening and the source areas.

One of the best ways to reduce reverberation times in the hall throughout the frequency range is to create niches in the wall surfaces behind and above the balconies. We then install a movable shade of absorptive material, operated by electromechanical means, that can be raised and lowered as desired. The face of the shade will absorb high-and mid-frequency sound, and low-frequency sound will be absorbed in the void between the shade and the wall. The beauty of this design is that the shade is fabricated from material that is the exact color of the wall surfaces and the visual aspect of the hall doesn't change when going from the classic mode to amplified popular programming.

Another approach would be to build a sound-transparent ceiling at a lower elevation and install a series of motor-operated tracks above it. Draperies would travel on these tracks and be deployed when amplified events were scheduled. One should build a series of hard cabinets in the upper space to house the gathered drapes during the classical concert mode. If everything above the sound-transparent ceiling is painted black and the audience house lighting is set at the same elevation as the false ceiling, audience members will not be able to see anything in the upper area of the room.

In a fan- or a reverse-fan-shaped room, this design solution is used in conjunction with a series of reflective forestage canopies placed over the first twelve rows of the audience. The overhead canopies are used to provide early reflections to the audience in the wider fan-shaped configuration. Some acousticians have even moved the main hard ceiling up and down to modify reverberation, but soft goods are still required on the side walls of such halls when amplification is used.

Just as important, we must deal with the stage or source area when amplified events are scheduled. This will entail bringing soft goods behind and to the side of performers of electronically reinforced shows. When amplified programs are presented, the acoustician must reduce the scattering of sound from the performer's monitor speakers that are normally set on the lip of the stage. These speakers are pointed at the performers to enable them to hear the other members of the group. Unfortunately, this positioning allows sound from the monitors to spill against the side and back wall of the stage, enter the reinforcement microphones to cause feedback, and ruin the musical balance and garble lyrics. Reflections from the low-frequency back wave of the main reinforcement speakers servicing the audience, energy from stage instrument amplifiers, and other incident sound reflections must be controlled.

Since the overhead orchestral reflectors do not provide complete coverage of the stage platform, there must be lift points for suspending velour draperies at the rear and side of the stage. The side wall surface over the seating balconies surrounding the stage should be made absorptive, similar to the surfaces in the audience listening area.

These are the elements that the physical acoustician can incorporate in his designs to modify the acoustic environment for amplified events. However, the sound-system designer must work in tandem with the acoustician and select speakers that will not spill reflections from the side walls of the hall. The acoustician should also add signal-delayed speakers to cover audiences at the rear of the hall so that the main arrays at the front of the stage don't overpower those seated within fifteen rows of the performance platform.

The architect and the owner may very well object aesthetically to the type of speakers needed to do the job. Once again, we see the need for the acoustician to stand firm on the acoustic requirements needed to satisfactorily present the client's programs. At times, acousticians, including myself, have made compromises on speaker designs for aesthetic reasons, only to have these decisions come back to haunt us after the building is finished.

You have now seen how a traditional nineteenth-century shoebox concert hall is designed. Design considerations for a surround concert hall are discussed in chapter 8.

SIX

MUSICAL MEMORY

"Perhaps, people who habitually listen to music in a certain hall . . . come to expect a musical style consonant with that hall and this expectation may bias their attitude towards other styles and other halls."

—Leo L. Beranek

Why does one concert hall sound good and another one poor? Why can one be revered while another is reviled? What are people hearing in such halls? What are the qualities that are being judged as musicians make music and audiences listen?

Over the last hundred years, many acoustical designers and architects copied the physical dimensions and construction materials of existing halls that were thought to be acoustically superior in an effort to replicate their acoustical qualities. Sometimes these halls were well accepted in their communities and sometimes they were not. Examples of concert halls modeled on the rectangular form that were not well received in their communities might be the Philharmonic Hall in New York and the Concert Hall at the Kennedy Center in Washington, D.C.

For us to understand this phenomenon, we have to look beyond the quantifiable physical measurements that are the backbone of acoustical practice to less tangible sound qualities, those related to personal preference. These qualities encompass subjective judgments on the part of the individuals—whether they are musicians, audience members, or conductors—and are based on the experience of hearing music performed in one or more environments over a period of years. It is a phenomenon that can best be termed "musical memory," and it is this "memory" that conditions people's listening experience and which we must be better able to define if we expect to build halls that are perceived as acoustically sound in a given community

In the concert experience, the listener is responding to the experience of hearing a composer's work through the medium of instrumental or vocal performance in a specific acoustic environment. What the listener is hearing is the physical event, which he or she perceives as the composer's and musician's art. Listening to a variety of compositions and musicians in the same environment over a long period of time will condition a listener to make his musical value judgments on the basis of just the musical work itself and/or the instrumentalist, rather than the space—which has remained constant in the equation.

Only when listeners change the concert environments in which they listen, keeping the repertoire and the ensembles relatively constant, does a new variable come into play to affect the listener's value judgments—the acoustic environment. Those who have spent a lifetime as professional listeners or as subscribers to programs in a particular hall or in halls of similar styles will find listening experiences in other spaces different. It is these differences that are interpreted as acoustic improvements or their opposite based on the listener's personal reference points.

This is the phenomenon that I call musical memory and which needs to be taken into account when designing the acoustics of new halls or renovating existing ones. Although the acoustician cannot ignore all the recently discovered psychoacoustic information regarding sensory perception that might enable him to develop new environments that can add to listening pleasure, he must also take musical memory into account.

This is probably more important when renovating a well-loved existing hall than when building a new one. However, would the criticism of the Philharmonic Hall have been as severe as it was without the community's acoustic memory of Carnegie Hall? Although it is true that some acoustical criteria in Philharmonic Hall fell outside prescribed tolerances, any new hall whose sound differed significantly from the familiar sound of Carnegie Hall would have had difficulty gaining acceptance in New York City at the time.

Understanding, analyzing, and describing musical memory is not an easy task. For example, take reverberation time—the time it takes sound to decay 60 decibels in a given space. The tolerance for acceptable mid-frequency-occupied reverberation time will run from 1.8 to 2.1 seconds for concert halls. Boston's Symphony Hall has an RT of 1.8 seconds; the Musikvereinssaal, 2.05 seconds; and Carnegie Hall, 1.7 seconds. The musical communities in each of these cities are fiercely partisan regarding the quality of sound produced in their respective halls. For this reason, we can assume that within the world community's tolerance band for acceptable listening criteria, there exist narrower such bands related to a local community's very specific musical memory.

Examples of musical memory abound. The New York musical community reacted strongly to some minor changes that were made in Carnegie Hall during the summer of 1966. A new hardwood floor was laid on the stage, the seats were replaced with their identical counterpart, and the stage was extended approximately three feet to provide more room for the large orchestral ensembles performing there. The explosive reaction of the New York musical community to these very minor physical changes was indicative of the acoustical sensitivity of experienced listeners who are acutely aware of the environmental characteristics of a specific space.

The resulting "more brilliant" acoustics of Carnegie Hall kept reappearing in almost every major music review that fall and as late as November 1967. Harold Schonberg, commenting on a concert by Vladimir Horowitz, wrote: "He had the piano slightly off and to the side trying to adjust to the more brilliant acoustics of the renovated Carnegie Hall. At that, there were some unpleasant pings in the treble. The piano? The hall? A combination of both? It is hard to say."

Much of the discussion regarding the changes in Carnegie Hall was not related to whether the new sound was better or worse, but rather to the fact that it was *different*. In fact, due to the commotion caused by the slight change to the familiar environment of Carnegie Hall, an extensive plan to renovate the stage area and the installation of a new organ that had been given to Carnegie Hall as a gift were both delayed and finally canceled. In September 1967, Julius Bloom, then executive director of Carnegie Hall, told Ted Strongin of the *New York Times* that the major reason for the delay was an effort to preserve the hall's famous mellowness. "We will go step by step," he said. "Whatever work we contemplate for the future will be pre-tested until there is 100% assurance it does not affect the hall's quality. This is an iron clad guarantee that Carnegie Hall makes."

Many years ago, I encountered a case of musical memory while conducting an evaluation rehearsal and survey for the Cincinnati Symphony prior to the renovation of the one-hundred-year-old Music Hall. The Cincinnati Music Hall, a 3,516-seat facility designed as a multiuse opera and symphonic hall, is a room that is sonically more like Carnegie Hall than like Vienna's Musikvereinssaal. It is warm and dark, but short on liveness due to a low ratio of volume to absorption in the hall, a condition that is further aggravated by the presence of a heavy, lined velour drapery (the main act teaser) that covers a large area of the proscenium opening.

To compensate for these conditions, we decided to evaluate the possibility of combining the volume of the stage house with that of the main hall in order to increase the ratio of volume to absorptive area and increase the room's liveness. This, in turn, would alter the acoustical characteristics of the Music Hall from those characteristic of a space somewhat similar to Carnegie Hall toward those of a space such as Boston's Symphony Hall, both of which were cited as halls with excellent acoustics.

No sooner had we raised the main act teaser two feet and increased coupling to the stage house than the change was apparent to conductor Max Rudolf and other members of the symphony staff. Their response to the different acoustical characteristic was negative, because their musical judgment had been conditioned by years of listening in the existing hall. Those not as close to the musical community of Cincinnati and less familiar with the sound of the hall found the brighter, reverberant field to their liking but were willing to concede that the velvet edge of the Music Hall acoustics was reduced as the curtain was drawn higher and higher.

One would be hard-pressed to determine whether the changes in the height of the main act teaser of the Music Hall improved or worsened the existing sound of the space, but changes occurred and the musical community felt uncomfortable with the unfamiliar sound. For this reason, Maestro Rudolf and the symphony manager decided to leave the curtain in its original position in order to maintain the familiar acoustic environment of the hall. Therefore, it became our responsibility throughout the renovation to see that none of the architectural changes modified the existing listening characteristics of the hall. Cincinnati's Music Hall falls well within the acceptable standard of the world community's judgment of proper concert environments. However, it was the decision of the local musical community to keep the environment within a much narrower band based on personal taste.

The controversy over the quality of orchestral sound at the Academy of Music in Philadelphia is another example of the unusual strength of musical memory. The Academy, long revered for its warm and intimate sound, was greatly disliked by Riccardo Muti, the music director who replaced Eugene Ormandy. Muti, whose personal preference was for a bright and live environment, pressed the orchestra to play in a style that did not complement the physical acoustic environment of the hall, and criticism of the acoustic quality of the space as well as that of the orchestra began to surface.

When Muti left, a new maestro, Wolfgang Sawallisch, came

on board. The *Philadelphia Inquirer* music critic Daniel Webster reported in 1995 that "European writers have noticed that Sawallisch has sought to return to something like the Ormandy sound, the burgundy resonance that has its roots in German repertoire and instrumental thinking." The sound Ormandy elicited from the orchestra was the one on which the acoustic reputation of the hall was based.

Very recently, the reopening of Jordan Hall in Boston after a major renovation brought dismay from the critics who felt that the sound had been ruined only because it had changed from what was familiar to what was unfamiliar.

What does all this mean, and how can it help architects, theater consultants, and acousticians design halls that meet the expectations of both the world and local communities? With the wide range of differences in sound of the various halls that are perceived as excellent, it might be reasonable to assume that there is no one perfect environment in which to play and listen to music. Given the subjective nature of musical memory and the situation-specific nature of its definition, one of the most dangerous things an acoustician can do is attempt to develop average criteria figures for halls defined as excellent throughout the world as a means of creating a new hall in a specific place that will incorporate all the criteria necessary for a single hall. The differences in the reflective patterns of the sound and the differences in the interrelationship of these patterns are what make excellent halls excellent yet individually different. These patterns produce a unique aural definition while still permitting the resulting acoustical characteristics to remain within acceptable worldwide standards. Attempting to average the criteria of these various halls will only destroy the very characteristics that originally created the familiar and therefore acceptable environment. Each community's standards are influenced by their specific listening environments. Experience clearly indicates that the averaging technique does not create a theoretically perfect musical space. It only results in producing average spaces that can't truly satisfy anyone.

Once we are willing to accept the concept that there is no perfect acoustical model and therefore no "perfect" hall, then it is up to the acoustician to work closely with the entire musical community of a given city to determine the acoustic characteristics that define listening pleasure in that community. Combining this information with an understanding of general psychoacoustic responses of listeners to reflection patterns, the acoustician can provide an individual community with an outstanding acoustic environment that will be accepted without reservation by musicians and audience alike.

Kennedy Center Concert Hall

The Kennedy Center Concert Hall, which opened in 1971, was billed as a true replica of the European shoebox design, a hall similar to those in Vienna, Leipzig, and Boston. This was the first single-purpose concert hall to be built after the fiasco of Philharmonic Hall, and although it opened to good reviews from the press, it soon became apparent that it was not up to the qualitative standards of the nineteenth-century shoeboxes.

Musicians had a hard time hearing themselves on stage, orchestral balances were off, and the audience felt that the hall was dry and deficient in bass energy. How could this be when the hall was touted as a copy of the nineteenth-century concert venues that were so beloved by musicians and audiences alike?

Well, the truth of the matter was quite simple. The hall was not a copy of the older facilities, and this observation delivers a warning to those who copy geometry. If you must copy nineteenth-century European-style rectangular halls, make sure you copy the interior as well as the outer geometric form.

After many years of working in this less-than-adequate acoustic environment, Kennedy Center management and the National Symphony decided it was time to make some acoustical improvements. When my firm was selected as the acoustic designer for the renovation of the hall, we found the following specific deficiencies:

John F. Kennedy Center for the Performing Arts Concert Hall, Washington D. C. The original stage area. Architect: Edward Durell Stone. Acoustics: Cyril M. Harris.

LISTENING AREA

1. The designers had added a third balcony to the room in order to increase seating capacity. The resulting additional absorption reduced mid- and bass-frequency reverberation times by eliminating the hard upper cap of the room where mid- and bass-frequency reverberations are normally generated.

    Measured reverberation at mid-frequency average was 1.7 seconds. This was lower than the European shoebox time of 2.0 seconds, but still within an acceptable range if all other reflecting patterns were within the desired ranges and the source area was well designed.

2. The hall was wider than the best European models, and people in the center of the orchestra seating area complained of a lack of presence and intimacy.

3. Echoes, coming off the hard nondiffusive rear wall of the hall, were annoying listeners seated nearest the stage in the second and third balconies.

Except for the echoes, which could easily have been removed, the listening area itself was a reasonable acoustic environment for the presentation of symphonic programs. The real musical acoustic problems were related to the source area: the stage and its surrounding surface areas.

SOURCE AREA

1. The stage geometry was very unconventional. It seemed to be a combination of the Symphony Hall orchestral platform and one of a European hall. The Boston stage platform is a traditional acoustic shell with the side walls and a sloping ceiling over the orchestra making a trapezoid, while the European halls were developed as the square end of a room with the side walls and stage ceiling as continuations of the audience chamber.

   The original Kennedy Center stage had trapezoidal side walls that fanned out at the midpoint of the platform, but the ceiling was a continuation of the room.

2. The original acoustician believed that exposed concert organs absorbed too much sound energy, and he designed wooden doors to slide out in front of the organ chambers when the instrument was not in use. The horn-like upstage portion of the platform, together with the hard surface of the sliding doors of the organ cover, emphasized the high-powered brass and percussion sections, while the strings, seated downstage where the side walls flared out, received fewer onstage early reflections and were overwhelmed by the more powerful brass and percussion instruments. Onstage hearing was poor, and many players wore ear plugs to prevent hearing loss.

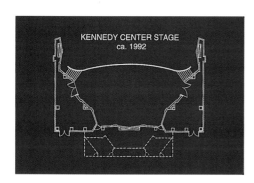

KENNEDY CENTER STAGE
ca. 1992

3. In addition the reduced bass-frequency reverberation times caused by the third balcony, the wooden doors covering the organ were light in weight and created a bass trap when closed in front of the air-filled organ chamber.

4. The wooden floor was laid directly over a concrete pad that eliminated key low-frequency resonant energy from the cellos and double basses.

Although we were confident we could resolve most of the acoustical anomalies in the hall, we were faced with the economic, political, and structural reality that the volume of the hall could not be increased due to the box-in-box construction that was developed to eliminate aircraft noise from nearby Reagan National Airport. The hall was structurally isolated from the outer frame of the building. By raising the ceiling, we would have ruptured the isolation characteristics of the hall, and we might as well have suggested that the planes land on the concert platform itself. The task at hand was to improve the acoustics without raising the ceiling, and this is what we did to accomplish our objective:

1. We increased the reverberation time throughout the frequency range by reducing the amount of absorption in the hall and adding reverberation chambers to the sides of the orchestra platform. We
   - eliminated half of the third-balcony seating area, creating a more reverberant upper hard cap to the room,
   - reupholstered the seats with less absorptive seat and back cushions,
   - removed the concrete substructure of the stage and installed a new wooden floor over an air space that allowed the metal pegs of the cellos and the double basses to set the floor into a resonant vibration,

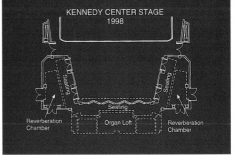

- modified spaces to the left and right of the stage platform to form reverberation chambers with long decays that coupled with the volume of the hall.

2. We provided excellent hearing conditions onstage and in the audience area and improved sectional balance. We
- reshaped the stage walls to project sound evenly to the musicians and the audience,
- uncovered the organ, which became an integral part of the room and reduced brass and percussion energy to the advantage of orchestral balance,
- constructed audience and choral seating around the stage platform to further reduce brass and percussion energy,
- installed a tunable reflector system over the orchestra and the first row of audience seating.

3. We eliminated echoes from the rear wall and the balcony fascias. We
- installed a small amount of absorptive material on the underside of balcony soffits closest to the rear wall.
- designed new diffusing balcony fascias.

John F. Kennedy Center for the Performing Arts Concert Hall Renovation, Washington, D. C. Redesigned stage area with open organ and stage reflectors. Architect: Quinn Evans; Acoustics: Jaffe Holden Scarbrough.

The changes dramatically improved the concert listening and performing experience. Leonard Slatkin, music director of the resident National Symphony, said. "It was as if the orchestra had been transformed . . . the strings play without forcing, the winds are transparent." James Oesterich, a music critic for the *New York Times*, wrote, "The sound remained resplendent . . . clear and expansive, yet blended and balanced."

Measurements taken in the hall revealed

interesting data. The reverberation time at mid frequency did not increase, though the low-frequency average gained 20 percent, which added a great deal of warmth to the hall. The bass ratio went from .90 to 1.1. The increase in the low-frequency response was due to the new coupling chambers and the new wooden floor over the air space.

The tunable overhead reflectors lowered the initial time delay gap to 20 milliseconds, providing early reflections to both the musicians and the patrons, resulting in better onstage hearing and increased intimacy and presence in the house. This corroborated some of our thinking in terms of mid-frequency reverberation time. If all other criteria meet required standards, halls with reverberation times less than 2.0 seconds and higher than 1.7 seconds can deliver the traditional European standard sonic experience. Remember, Boston's Symphony Hall, Carnegie Hall, and Severance Hall have all been measured at 1.8 seconds or less at mid frequency.

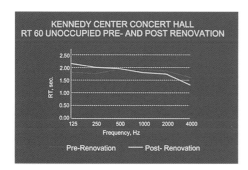

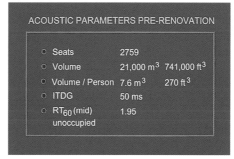

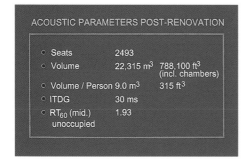

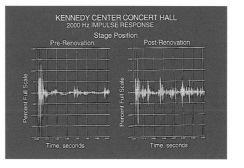

SEVEN

RECITAL HALLS

The acoustic intimacy of a space is largely based on the delay between the direct sound and the first reflections. A short delay provides a greater sense of intimacy. This quality comes naturally in a small space, where the walls and ceiling are relatively close to the audience, but it is harder to achieve in a large room.

—Dawn Schuette and Lawrence Kirkegaard

The key to designing a successful hall is to make sure the client has a clear understanding of the program use of the space.

Some recital halls, usually those at universities and colleges, might plan to use the space for symphonic programs as well as for smaller ensembles and soloists. These school orchestras may not exceed seventy players, sometimes performing along with a chorus of one hundred, but the acoustician will still have to develop an environment suitable for a larger ensemble, since it's almost certain that the brass, horn, and percussion sections will be the same size as those in a professional orchestra of a hundred players (due to the traditional orchestration of symphonic works), and the loudness of those sections will drive the design of the hall.

A recital hall must be designed to accommodate the power levels of the ensembles using the space regardless of the seating capacity.

Let's take the example of an 800-seat recital hall at a music conservatory or at a school of music at a major university. The design team is told that the new recital hall must accommodate both the organization's symphonic program and the smaller ensembles associated with such a space.

In this instance, we might like to develop a reverberation time at mid frequency of 2.0 seconds, a figure equal to that of many of the best-loved symphonic venues. However, the longer we extend reverberation in a recital hall, the more difficult it will be to obtain clarity for small ensembles and soloists performing Bach fugues or Mozart quartets. Sixty-fourth notes can run together and turn to mush in a hall with too extended a reverberation time. However, knowing that Boston's Symphony Hall, Severance Hall, and Carnegie Hall, all much-admired halls, have reverberation times at mid frequency averaging between 1.7 and 1.8 seconds, we might decide to set our design goal in the lower range.

A 2,000-seat contemporary shoebox symphonic hall designed for a professional orchestra might require about 225 cubic feet (6.4 cubic meters) per seat or 450,000 cubic feet (12,600 cubic meters) total volume in the hall in order to achieve a mid-frequency average reverberation time of 1.7 seconds. This will also provide sufficient air volume to accommodate the power of a large orchestra and choir so that the sound will not become shrill. Air absorbs high frequencies, so we must have enough volume to cut down the highs and keep the bass ratio high.

If you want an 800-seat recital hall to achieve a 1.7-second reverberation time, you have to provide about 176,800 cubic feet (5,006 cubic meters) of volume. This would achieve the 1.7-second reverberation goal, but would not provide enough air volume to prevent the orchestral sound from become harsh. In my experience, you must increase the volume of an 800-seat recital hall to at least 350,000 cubic feet (9,910 cubic meters) and then develop a design that will allow you bring the reverberation time down to the original desired goal.

This can be done by adding absorption in the upper cap of the room or by designing the hall in a T configuration, such as the 400-seat Spivey Hall at Clayton State University near Atlanta or the 800-seat Belding Theater at the Bushnell Center in Hartford, Connecticut. Spivey is considered one of the best recital halls in the country and was designed by Rein Pirn of the acoustical consulting firm of Acentech in Cambridge, Massachusetts. By manipulating drapes in the T-shaped hall, one can go from chamber works to large-scale organ recitals in an acoustical environment that approximates that of many Gothic cathedrals. In the stage area, you will have to allow 2,000 square feet (186 square meters) for the orchestra and another 1,500 feet (457 meters) for side stages or audience seating if you are planning to wrap the orchestra platform with audience seating.

In many instances, schools will want to build a multiuse hall that will accommodate theater, opera, and dance productions as well as orchestral performances. In those cases, the acoustician might design the hall with less air volume and couple the stage house to increase the reverberation time. The stage house volume will absorb some of the high-powered brass and percussion energy, so you won't have to worry about creating the harsh symphonic sound that would occur in the single-purpose space if you reduced the air volume. Bear in mind that in these multiuse recital halls, we are still using coupled tunable orchestra shells.

Achieving proper sectional balance is more difficult when working with smaller orchestras, since the reduction in the number of players is usually concentrated in the string sections, the least powerful group of the symphonic instruments. Most scores won't let you cut the number of brass, percussion, and woodwind players. In the single-purpose hall, the acoustician may suggest the installation of an organ behind the orchestra or place permanent soft seats there for choristers or audience members during nonchoral concerts to dampen these louder sections.

If the client is building a recital hall in a city or on a university campus that already has adequate concert rooms for orchestral

Pepsico Recital Hall, Texas Christian University, Fort Worth, Texas. First concert hall coupled to an exterior volume; Architect: Hardy, Holzman, Pfeiffer Associates. Acoustics: Jaffe Holden Scarbrough.

performances, then he or she can specify a much smaller stage platform and reduce air volume to achieve an average mid-frequency reverberation time of 1.3 to 1.5 seconds. Such rooms might be built in conjunction with museums, corporate offices, music conservatories, multifacility performing arts centers, or ethnic cultural centers. In

New York, one can find such rooms at the Metropolitan Museum of Art, Carnegie Hall, the New York Times Building, the Juilliard School of Music, the 92nd Street Y, and the Society for Ethical Culture.

One of the most interesting nonsymphonic concert halls I have worked on was at Texas Christian University in Fort Worth. The hall itself is built in the middle of a reverberant chamber with openings in the walls and ceiling of the room.

The concept for this design came on a plane ride from Texas with architect Malcolm Holzman of Hardy Holzman Pfeiffer Architects. Creative architects will challenge the acoustician to respond to innovative design concepts. Sometimes the laws of physics negate these ideas, but I have always tried to accommodate those concepts I thought viable within the constraints of providing outstanding acoustic environments.

Malcolm Holzman and Frank Gehry, with whom I worked on the Hollywood Bowl, are two architects who have, on occasion, pushed me to the limit. Gehry wanted to know if I could design a shell out of cardboard and a symphonic music pavilion without an acoustic hard cap roof (see chapter 11), and it was Holzman who asked me if I could design an acoustic shell that would enclose both the musicians and the audience.

The outer volume of the TCU space was set in a hard masonry box, and the interior shell was built of dense composition board. Traveling draperies were positioned in both the upper volume of the chamber and in the space surrounding the performance platform and the audience. It took the students and the faculty a little time to realize that the outer volume at stage level had to be treated like a wing space in a theater. Absolute quiet was required, and no warming up on instruments, please.

Another Holzman recital hall at Middlebury College in Vermont turned out extremely well and formed the basis for designs we utilized in Columbus, Georgia, and Houston, Texas. The Middlebury design followed concept of the surround halls by extending a

*Mahaney Center for the Arts
Concert Hall, Middlebury
College, Middlebury,
Vermont, Surround-style
concert hall. Architect:
Hardy, Holzman, Pfeiffer
Associates. Acoustics: Jaffe
Holden Scarbrough.*

Bennett•Gordon Hall, Ravinia Music Festival, Highland Park, Illinois. Coupled space recital hall. Architect: Lubotsky Metter Worthington & Law. Acoustics: Jaffe Acoustics.

single row of balcony seating around three-quarters of the room (see chapter 8). At the rear of the stage platform, additional rows were added to the balcony to accommodate the chorus or additional audience seating for nonchoral concerts.

Two other recital halls that incorporate unique design solutions should be mentioned here: Bennett•Gordon Hall at the Stearns Institute for Young Artists at Ravinia and Zankel Hall, the underground recital space in Carnegie Hall.

Bennett•Gordon Hall at Ravinia Festival Park was programmed to hold master classes for young professionals during the summer months. In the winter, it becomes a musical performance center for the community of Highland Park, Illinois. I designed the stage end of the space as I might have approached an outdoor music pavilion.

We built a 200,000-cubic-foot (5,663-cubic-meter) box with a 40-foot (12-meter) ceiling. Within the box, we designed a tunable coupled shell (see chapter 9) with one difference: the side panels were able to pivot and we could adjust the amount of side coupling the way we had been treating ceiling units since the 1960s. In addition, these side shell towers could become hard wings for modest dance and opera productions.

Zankel Hall is a story in itself. It is a single-purpose room that was carved out of the solid rock of Manhattan Island; see case study that follows.

Zankel Hall

Zankel Hall was one of my strangest assignments. Located in the basement of Carnegie Hall directly under the world-renowned Isaac Stern Auditorium, it was to be designed to house one of the most diverse musical programs in history.

Brainchild of the late Judith Aaron, former executive director of Carnegie Hall, and Isaac Stern, the savior of the hall when it was about to be torn down so as not to compete with the soon-to-be-completed Philharmonic Hall at Lincoln Center, the program for the space encompassed classical recital fare, contemporary music, world music, jazz, pop, master classes, themed festivals, and lectures.

When Carnegie Hall was built in the late 1890s, the basement of the building was designed as a traditional concert hall for small classical ensembles and soloists. Unfortunately, state-of-the-art acoustical isolation was not well developed, and it was impossible to schedule concerts simultaneously in the upper and lower halls. Also, the volume of the space was too low for many classical ensembles. Thus, management rented the space to the American Academy of Dramatic Arts, and for years the space functioned as a teaching studio and a showcase for young performers.

Subsequently, the room was converted to an art cinema, the Little Carnegie, and proper isolation was achieved by suspending a new sound-isolation ceiling in the space and mounting acoustical absorptive material on the walls. That a large amount of volume was eliminated from the space and fuzz added to the room did not matter, because classical music was no longer performed in the space.

In 2000, the management of Carnegie Hall embarked on plans to convert the existing cinema back to a recital hall, but one with a vastly different program. James Polshek & Partners were selected as the architects, Auerbach Pollock Friedlander as the theater consultants, and I as acoustic consultant.

The acoustic problems were myriad. The volume of the space was too low for classical music presentations, the isolation between halls without the secondary ceiling was unsatisfactory, and the 57th Street subway station was positioned 10 feet from the structural wall of the main building. In addition, the client wanted to be able to mount performances on a typical end stage of a shoebox-style room but at the same time provide a way to place artists in the middle of the room for arena-style events.

Plan of Judy and Arthur Zankel Hall at Carnegie Hall, New York N.Y. A 599-seat recital hall located under Carnegie's main Stern Auditorium. Architects: Polshek Partnership. Acoustics: Jaffe Holden.

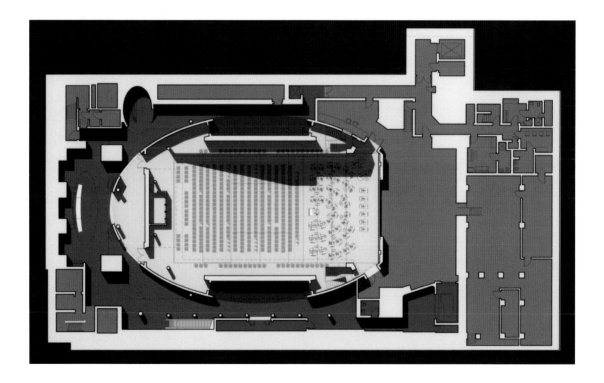

Carnegie Hall sits on a rise of Manhattan granite, and we had to dig out 20 feet of rock to gain the volume needed for the hall to be successful. Even the removal of this amount of rock left us a little shy of the volume necessary for large classical music ensembles. However, large groups of musicians were not scheduled to perform here, and slightly lower reverberation times were perfect for contemporary and world music, amplified jazz, pop, lectures, and conferences. Because we would be shy on air volume, we added diffuser panels to the side and end walls of the hall to help balance high- and low-frequency reverberation and to reduce harshness.

When we removed the dropped ceiling installed in the cinema, we found that the grout between the brick arches supporting the orchestra floor of Stern Hall had crumbled away in many spots. These had to be resealed as the first step in developing the required isolation in the new concert venue. Since I was looking for the maximum volume possible, we could not develop a typical dropped-ceiling design with a large air space between isolation layers. Instead, we designed a dense, multilayered secondary ceiling hung from another dense membrane positioned directly under the arches. We left only enough room for electrical wiring in the space between the layers.

Auerbach Pollock Friedlander positioned elevator lifts over a major portion of the hall area together with rolling seating dollies that could be stored in an open space behind the end wall of the hall. This enabled the owners to move from an end stage presentation to one mounted in the center of the room.

Reducing subway noise was the most difficult part of the assignment. The station was extremely close to the hall, and a low level of subway noise could always be heard on the audience-right side of Stern Auditorium. Even with the elimination of beams that supported the sidewalk on Seventh Avenue and the cooperation of the Metropolitan Transit Authority in modifying the track supports, one can still detect a bit of a rumble when a train leaves the station. However, by cutting the beams under the sidewalk, we did eliminate the last vestiges of subway noise in Stern Auditorium.

Zankel Hall has lived up to its potential. Performances of Bach, Mozart, and Haydn are regularly scheduled alongside those of Lou Harrison, John Adams, and Karlheinz Stockhausen. African, Asian, and Latin American music have drawn sellout crowds. The chamber hall acoustics of Zankel are well suited to the innovative programming of the hall management.

Judy and Arthur Zankel Hall, Carnegie Hall, New York, N.Y. Rendering of hall in the surround mode. Architect: Polshek Partnership Architects. Acoustics: Jaffe Holden.

With the addition of some draperies on the back wall of the stage as well as at the rear corners of the hall, the acoustic environment becomes appropriate for amplified programming. The venue is equipped with a wide variety of contemporary technology to link its program with other sites throughout the world. One of the most moving musical experiences I have encountered was a joint concert of the Boys and Girls Choirs of Harlem singing "We Shall Overcome" in synchronization with a children's choir from Johannesburg, South Africa. The Harlem choirs were on the Zankel stage, and the African choir was projected on a giant screen behind the local musicians. I am not ashamed to say I was in tears.

EIGHT

NEW SURROUND STYLE

As scheduled, Italy's haute couture designers got to flaunt their ingenuity at cantilevering and buttressing. Perfumed waves of mostly aged Milanese; the presidents of Italy, Greece, Germany, and Austria; the sheik of Qatar; and pomaded bankers carting tickets priced up to $2,900 arrived under the glare of spotlights and television cameras . . .

—Michael Kimmelman

Concert halls and opera houses—what they are and what they project—seem to be very important factors in attracting and repelling different sectors of the public. On the positive side, they are the acoustical environment for which much of the traditional symphonic and operatic repertoire has been written. In terms of orchestral presentations, great pains are taken during the design stages of concert hall construction to achieve a sound comparable to the familiar listening standard established by the narrow rectangular halls constructed in Europe during the nineteenth century. Although it has been proven that the relationship of reflecting patterns in a hall rather than some specific architectural style is responsible for obtaining a satisfactory end result, many in the musical community are not aware of this fact or stubbornly refuse to believe it.

Architecturally, concert halls reflect the performing spaces of past eras when orchestras played for kings, queens, and their courts. Opulence and grandeur are still highly valued by a major segment of present-day audiences, perhaps as an opportunity for vicarious participation in the celebrations and rituals characteristic of the past. Socially, the hall itself stands as a permanent and visual symbol of the cultural sophistication of the community.

The propagation of these traditional values is a partial reason for the refusal of many music lovers to attend events in these facilities. Major segments of our population, such as the young and the working class, are turned off by the ceremony, the formalistic response expected by the cognoscenti, and the high cost of good seats.

This attitude of knowledgeable superiority has had a debilitating effect on developing audiences for classical music events. Orchestras throughout the country are struggling financially and desperately trying to entice new and younger audiences to the concert hall. After years of resisting changes in the relationship between performer and audience in symphony halls, they now seem ready to embrace new environments.

This change in attitude evolved over a period of many years, starting with the success of the summer music festivals at Tanglewood in Lenox, Massachusetts, and Ravinia in Highland Park, Illinois—summer homes of the Boston and Chicago symphonies respectively—and continuing in the decisions in 1965 by the Metropolitan Opera to hold concert versions of opera at Lewisohn Stadium in New York City and by the New York Philharmonic to create a touring stage and shell for concerts to be held in every borough of the city.

In the 1970s, a few innovative members of the musical community were searching for ways to encourage new and younger audiences to attend classical music concerts. Nancy Hanks, director of the National Endowment for the Arts, agreed to have the organization sponsor a research project entitled "Environments and the Concert Experience." This study was undertaken by Professor Larry Medlin, professor of light-weight structures at Washington University, and

me in conjunction with the Saint Louis Symphony, whose executive director, Peter Pastreich, was receptive to the idea. The study would explore the possibilities of presenting free orchestral concerts on the plaza of an upscale suburban shopping mall, in the Saint Louis Blues Arena (hockey), in the Union Station railroad terminal, in a limestone cavern having the same reverberation time as the Musikvereinesaal in Vienna, and in the park under the Gateway Arch.

The grant from the Endowment enabled the research team to present a number of free, experimental, informal concerts of the Saint Louis Symphony on the plaza of the Clayton Mall and under the Gateway Arch. The concert at the mall was performed under a cloth structure constructed from a stretch fabric material used to manufacture women's underwear, shaped into position with

Pierre Boulez conducting the New York Philharmonic Orchestra in an informal rug concert at Lincoln Center, 1974.

Saint Louis Symphony performing under a stretch fabric tensile membrane structure at the Clayton Mall, Clayton, Missouri. Project designer: Larry Medlin. Acoustics: Jaffe Acoustics.

basketballs and supported by guy wires. In the symphony concert at the Gateway Arch park, the audience was immersed in electronically simulated concert hall reflections similar to those found in indoor rooms. The multiple loudspeakers used for this concert were supported by cable trusses running from stage towers to a ring of telephone poles at the rear of the audience seating area. These concerts were well received and supported the concept that there was an audience for less formal al fresco symphonic performances. The Saint Louis Symphony subsequently acquired a portable stage similar in concept to the one pioneered by the New York Philharmonic and presented free outdoor concerts throughout the area.

Saint Louis wasn't the only city opening new doors. A few years later, Peter Wexler, the well-known opera scenic designer, and Pierre Boulez, conductor of the New York Philharmonic Orchestra at the time, removed all the seats in Lincoln Center's Philharmonic Hall, placed rugs on the floor, and invited students from universities throughout the city to attend an orchestral concert at a nominal charge. The hall was sold out at concert time and many had to be turned away.

Not to be outdone, Ernest Fleischmann, the executive director of the Los Angeles Philharmonic, staged a joint concert of his orchestra with Frank Zappa and the Mothers of Invention in the Pauley Pavilion at the University of California, Los Angeles, another sold-out event.

Although all of these concerts were innovative and well attended by younger enthusiastic audiences, they failed to bring these new potential listeners back to the formal concert halls during the regular subscription seasons. Why were these efforts unsuccessful? Was

Philharmonie, Berlin, Germany. Pioneering concept of the "vineyard-style" hall. Note the many terraces and the low frequency absorbers on the ceiling. Architect: Hans Scharoun. Acoustics: Lothar Cremer.

Kammermusiksaal der
Philharmonie, Berlin,
Germany. Second Berlin
hall in the "vineyard style."
Architect: Edgar Wisniewski.
Acoustics: Lothar Cremer.

it the environment? Was it the high ticket cost of the indoor concert hall event? Were new patrons fearful that they would be embarrassed by showing up dressed inappropriately or caught applauding between movements?

About the same time, Eric Marden, reporting on a study of audience attitudes for the Ford Foundation, predicted a 20 percent increase in attendance at concerts, operas, and ballets if audiences could be persuaded that these events were not formal, stuffy affairs attended and sponsored by a wealthy elite.

The Marden report and these experiences made a strong case for the more intimate surround hall. If new audiences were attracted to the informality of concert experiences in familiar environments such as a park, a basketball arena, a shopping mall plaza or a concert hall

THE ACOUSTICS OF PERFORMANCE HALLS

that had been doctored to create an indoor lawn, why not design new concert halls to be less formal, more friendly, spaces?

The first individuals to take the plunge were the architect Hans Scharoun and the acoustician Lothar Cremer in 1963. With most concert halls and opera houses in Germany destroyed during the Second World War, the Berlin Philharmonic, among others, needed a new facility and Scharoun was selected as the designer. Rather than revert to the formal architectural style of the privileged classes of earlier centuries, Scharoun wanted to create a more egalitarian hall, in keeping with the desires of the new progressive German postwar society.

He took as his model the open-air band concerts that had been held in European village squares for centuries. Audiences surround the performers placed on a platform or bandstand in the middle of the square, and people listen to the concert at ground level and from balconies overlooking the square. Cremer was somewhat hesitant to break with the shoebox tradition, but relying on the theory that reflected energy, not geometry, was the key to developing the traditional symphonic sound, he agreed to take on the assignment.

The result of the work of these two innovative pioneers was the Berlin Philharmonie, one of the most successful new concert halls in the world and the model for all the subsequent surround halls that were built in New Zealand, Mexico, the United States, Japan, and Europe over the next fifty years.

How were Scharoun and Cremer able to create the traditional sound in a hall with such different geometric plans? Let's think of the Beranek trio, the reflections that relate to the familiar concert listening experience—e.g., initial time delay gap, reverberation at mid frequencies, and reverberation at low frequencies.

To provide a portion of the audience with the familiar experience of sitting in a more traditional geometry, the designers placed several hundred patrons directly in front of the performance platform and surrounded this area with high seating terraces. Enclosed by the walls of these terraces, patrons in this area received early reflections

*Sala Nezahualcóyotl,
Universidad Nacional
Autónoma de Mexico,
Mexico City. Note the
extensive reflector system
over the stage. Architect:
Orso Nuñez & Arcadio Artis.
Acoustics: Jaffe Acoustics*

within the 20- to 30-millisecond period needed for intimacy, pres-ence, and definition. In this specific location, one might say they created a hall within a hall. Upper terraces positioned at different heights were located around the stage in a 280-degree pattern and, together with slanting tentlike ceilings, provided early reflections for those seated in these locations. In addition, they suspended reflector panels from the ceiling to enhance presence for those patrons seated beyond the range of reflections coming from terrace walls and ceil-ing surfaces. Onstage, they created hard reflective side walls of thick wood that, together with the overhead reflectors, enabled the musi-cians to hear themselves and other members of the ensemble as well as to blend the orchestral sound.

Since the bowl-like absorptive audience would tend to soak up more sound than listeners in a shoebox hall, the team added more volume to the upper reaches of the hall beyond the highest seating terraces. This enhanced both low- and mid-frequency reverberation. An interesting innovation was the incorporation of tunable low-frequency absorbers in the ceiling of the hall, which are patches of sound-absorbing material.

With a portion of the audience behind and to the side of the performance platform, the overall loudness of the ensemble was slightly reduced, although the ratio of the direct orchestral sound to reverberation field was similar to those found in the rectangular halls, and all other necessary criteria were in place to create the traditional and familiar symphonic environment.

The measurements of key criteria in the Philharmonie matched those of the best-received shoebox halls, and the positive responses of audience to the less formal concert environment gave acousticians confidence in altering the geometry of newer halls to represent more egalitarian values.

In the 1970's several acousticians interested in providing more egalitarian spaces began to design surround halls. Harold Marshall designed the Town Hall Auditorium in Christchurch, New Zealand; I worked on the Sala Nezahualcóyotl in Mexico City and Boettcher Hall in Denver; and Peter De Lange provided acoustical input on the Muziekcentrum Vredenburg in Utrecht, The Netherlands.

In the last twenty-five years, the majority of new concert halls in Japan and Europe have opted for the surround style, although it is only recently that American orchestras are beginning to appreciate the advantage of these facilities (the new Disney Hall in Los Angeles, for one).

There were some earlier models for surround halls before the Berlin Philharmonic. A number of nineteenth- and early-twentieth-century European halls, such as the Concertgebouw in Amsterdam, had a more square geometry with a large number of patrons sitting to the side and behind the orchestra platform. Others, including the Usher Hall in Edinburgh, Scotland; Colston Hall in Bristol, England, and St. Andrew's Hall in Glasgow, Scotland, had seats for a

*The Musiekcentrum
Vradenburg Utrecht, The
Netherlands. Another
surround hall. This one
has a triple glass skylight
over the stage to provide
light and eliminate street
sound. Architect: Herman
Hertzberger. Acoustics:
Peter DeLange.*

THE ACOUSTICS OF PERFORMANCE HALLS

full symphony chorus behind the performance platform, that could be sold to audience members during nonchoral concerts.

The more intimate relationship between performer and audience in a surround hall has become a viable alternative, and the musical community has taken this form to heart.

Listed below is a table of quantitative measurements of surround halls compared to the traditional shoebox design, along with qualitative comments.

AVERAGE MID-FREQUENCY REVERBERATION TIME IN HALLS OF DIFFERENT GEOMETRY			
HALL	CITY	GEOMETRY	SECONDS
Concertgebouw	Amsterdam	rectangle	2.0
Grosser Musikvereinssaal	Vienna	rectangle	2.0
Boston Symphony Hall	Boston	rectangle	1.9
Berlin Phiharmonie	Berlin	surround	2.0
Sala Nezahualcóyotl	Mexico City	surround	2.0
Suntory Hall	Tokyo	surround	2.0
Bass Performance Hall	Fort Worth, TX	horseshoe	2.0
Tanglewood	Lenox, MA	fan	1.9

NINE

MULTIPURPOSE PERFORMANCE HALLS

Most city governments cannot afford to build a concert hall *and* a theater and opera house. They must somehow make do with a performance space that can meet all the demands reasonably. The only way these objectives can be accomplished is by having a variable architecture that produces variable acoustics.

—Robert E. Apfel

In the United States during the early and mid twentieth century, we did not have the luxury of building single-purpose orchestra halls. The symphonic tradition was not as strong in America as it was in Europe, and symphony organizations, which were almost entirely privately funded, could not afford to construct their own one-room facilities and so were forced to play in multipurpose venues such as vaudeville houses, film theaters, and high school and college auditoriums. Only a small number of symphonies performed in one-room dedicated concert facilities—in 1960, only the orchestras of Boston, New York, Chicago, Cleveland, Buffalo, and New Haven, and perhaps a handful of lesser-known smaller ensembles.

Orchestras forced to perform in multipurpose rooms played in modified box sets of plywood and canvas shaped to form an acoustical shell. In order to project sound through the proscenium opening, the side walls were tapered toward the rear of the stage and the roof of the box was angled upward. In some instances, a set of drapery curtains was hung behind the ensemble to hide the ugly rear walls of these theaters.

During the late 1950s and throughout the next three decades, the American economy grew rapidly, and many cities built new performing arts centers to enhance their civic image and satisfy the diverse cultural aspirations of the local population. The focal point of most of these centers was a large, multiple-purpose performance hall, seating between 2,500 and 3,000 people, that was intended to serve both as a home for the city's orchestra, opera company, and ballet troupe, and a site for touring Broadway musicals, popular music concerts, and a variety of other forms of entertainment.

A lot of these halls were designed for optimum theatrical sight lines rather than symphonic acoustics and were wide fan-shaped rooms. Many of them had multiple deep balconies that acoustically shaded those seated below. The Ford Auditorium in Detroit and Jesse Jones Hall in Houston respectively are examples of these designs. With the high absorption factor of the large audience in relation to the available volume, the reverberation times in these theaters were lower than desirable for symphonic events.

Was it really physically possible to design a multipurpose hall that could satisfy the acoustical requirements of all these different user groups, from symphony orchestras to amplified Broadway musical theater? For almost all of the multipurpose halls designed during this period, the answer was no. The designers of the period attempted to find a middle ground by averaging the acoustical criteria for speech and music. The results, however, were unsatisfactory for both classical events and for amplified popular programs. Audiences found the rooms too dead for satisfactory symphonic listening, and amplified Broadway theater and popular programs lacked speech clarity. The "middle of the road" acoustical characteristics of many of these early multipurpose halls led users

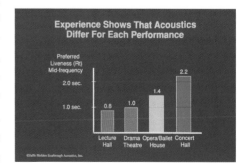

and audiences to conclude that a multipurpose hall was, in fact, a "no-purpose" hall.

Being aware of the symphonic acoustic problems in these large multiuse halls, many architectural acoustic designers attempted to resolve the difficulties by designing massive contained acoustic enclosures of steel that were placed in the stage houses of these theaters to increase reverberation times for orchestral events. The structural engineers on the projects had to reinforce the buildings to support the weight of these massive concert shells. To accommodate opera, amplified Broadway musicals, and popular music programs, these structures were removed from the stage by electromechanical means, and draperies were dropped along the walls of the halls to reduce reverberation times for better speech intelligibility.

This design innovation improved the capabilities of the multi-

Broward Center for the Performing Arts, Ft Lauderdale, Florida. Typical fan-shaped, multipurpose hall. Architect: Benjamin Thompson Associates. Acoustics: Kirkegaard & Associates.

THE ACOUSTICS OF PERFORMANCE HALLS

purpose hall, but it didn't provide the traditional symphonic sound of the one-room European concert hall. The heavy, contained concert shell, shaped like a horn, tended to emphasize the high-powered brass and percussion instruments positioned in front of the rear wall, in the throat of the enclosure, over the lower-powered strings, throwing sections of the orchestra out of balance. The problem was not a new one; even in the best-loved single-room European halls, one can occasionally see the violas and cellos bowing away and not hear them at all when the brass and percussion take over. I had this experience at the Grosser Musikvereinssaal in Vienna listening to a performance of Schubert's Unfinished Symphony, when the hard choral seats behind the orchestra were empty and could not absorb the high sound levels of the brass and percussion. In a multipurpose hall with a contained shell, this happened all the time. In addition, the reduced air volume over the orchestra in these heavy contained shells did not permit orchestral energy to dissipate naturally and, as a result, the sound acquired a hard and harsh quality.

The time seemed ripe for a new approach to shell design, and I was fortunate to be in the right place at the right time. In the 1950s, I had a small engineering firm that specialized in the design of lightweight equipment for theater and television. Our work included building a removable magnesium floor for Sid Caesar's *Show of Shows* when the company temporarily leased a Broadway theater, and constructing lightweight magnesium and fiberglass scenic flats for the original Broadway production of *Black Nativity*.

It was in the late fifties that Boris Goldovsky, director of the New England Opera Theatre and the Tanglewood Opera Workshop, approached me and asked if I would be interested in designing and building a prototype of a lightweight concert shell that might resolve the acoustical problems he had encountered while touring his opera company throughout the United States. If successful, the shells would be designed, fabricated, and installed by my engineering firm. Having studied the violin for seven years and played in a student orchestra, I was somewhat conversant in the subject and agreed to give it a try.

The story of the development of this shell is quite interesting. Charles Munch, music director of the Boston Symphony Orchestra, was asked to perform a holiday concert under the vaulted roof of the Boston Garden, home to the ice-skating Bruins and the basketball-playing Celtics. Maestro Munch was very concerned that the cavernous acoustics of the space would turn orchestral sound to mush. Goldovsky had already experimented with fiberglass panels with his touring opera productions, and Munch asked him to lend this equipment to the BSO for the Boston Garden concert to help focus the sound. Goldovsky agreed, and the concert was acoustically successful. If a number of lightweight fiberglass wall panels surrounding an orchestra in a sports arena could improve the symphonic environment, Goldovsky wondered what a real concert shell might do for orchestras in the multipurpose movie theaters and high school auditoriums used by so many symphonic ensembles.

After accepting the challenge to design a shell for Goldovsky's opera, I started researching the existing state of affairs. The canvas and plywood box sets used by many orchestras were unwieldy units with limited ability to provide reading light for the musicians. Some of these shells were elaborately painted, like scenic drops, to give the impression that the orchestra was performing in a palace ballroom or an outdoor garden. Most, however, were simply given a coat of paint and thrown together on concert day with the highly absorptive main act curtain filling in the open space between the downstage edge of the ceiling and the plaster proscenium face. These shells did little to balance the sections of the orchestra and allowed low-frequency energy to be lost in the high reaches of the stage house. The upper frequencies of the string and woodwind sounds were enhanced by the single ceilings of these units, and onstage hearing for the musicians was improved. However, the loss of low-frequency energy reduced warmth, and the result was a sound with extremely low levels of viola, cello, and bass viol.

The alternative to these canvas and plywood boxes was the heavy contained wooden or steel shells, moved by electric winches, that increased reverberation but unbalanced sections and created a harsh sound because of the reduced air volume over the orchestra. Many musicians claimed they found it difficult to hear one another in these contained shells with a single sloped ceiling. It seemed to me that if I could create a new shell that combined the best characteristics of the canvas and the contained shell and eliminated the problems of both, I might be able to produce an environment in a multipurpose theater that would come close to satisfying the qualitative judgments of the musical community.

The first step was to develop a ceiling design of individual panels that could be suspended from the existing counterweighted rigging systems that are standard in almost all multipurpose auditoriums to this day. Three ceiling sections, approximately 8 feet (2.4 meters) in width, would be positioned parallel to the stage apron and would reinforce the individual sections of the orchestra. Since a typical orchestral arrangement places the high and low strings downstage, the woodwinds behind them, and the brass and percussion at the rear of the platform, three individual ceilings would cover the entire ensemble. If the piece called for a chorus, a fourth ceiling could be added to the design. There was a 2-foot (0.6-meter) gap between the ceilings. This allowed the acoustician to position the ceilings to balance the power outputs of the various sections and to place reading-light fixtures in the openings.

An important feature of these ceilings was that they were hinged along the center line to create two different reflecting angles in each individual ceiling unit. This enabled the designer to tune the shell so that a portion of the sound energy

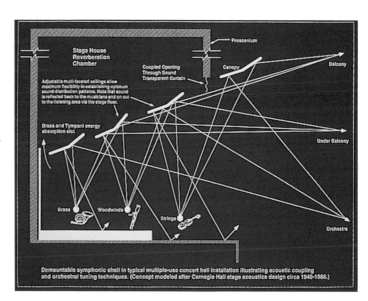

Demountable symphonic shell in typical multiple-use concert hall installation illustrating acoustic coupling and orchestral tuning techniques. (Concept modeled after Carnegie Hall stage acoustics design circa 1940–1986.)

reflected from these surfaces would be directed toward the audience and another portion returned to the musicians on stage.

The wall sections of the shell were designed as typical theatrical flats lashed together with standard theatrical hardware and arranged in an accordion pleat to help diffuse and blend the sound of the ensemble. These standing panels varied in height from 14 feet (4.3 meters) to 24 feet (7.3 meters), depending on the height of the proscenium opening. The face material was 1/16-inch (1.39-centimenter) laminated fiberglass sheet and weighed .5 pound per square foot (2.53 kilos per square meter) . They were light enough for the stage crews to set by hand.

With this design in mind, I formed a company called Stagecraft Corporation in partnership with an aluminum fabricator in Peekskill, New York, who built the units. The New England Opera Theatre

Corning Symphony, in a Stagecraft orchestra shell at the Corning Glass Center. Shell designer: Christopher Jaffe.

THE ACOUSTICS OF PERFORMANCE HALLS

was to receive a royalty on each shell, since we were relying on Mr. Goldovsky's contacts in the music world to get the project moving.

The prototype was constructed, and we conducted preliminary tests at the Opera Workshop at Tanglewood. All went well with the tests, but we were having difficulty making an initial sale. Most of our client base was having trouble meeting musicians' salaries, and the idea of spending thousands of dollars for a stage shell wasn't in their budgets. At this point, I had an idea. We had a prototype; why not offer to rent the shell or parts of it to orchestras and see if we could not gain more credibility? Three rentals opened the door for our firm, a set of ceilings for a gymnasium at the Iowa State University in Ames, a set of standing panels for the Norwalk Symphony in Connecticut, and a complete shell for the Corning Glass Works Auditorium in Corning, New York. After testing the shell in their performances, all three organizations purchased our equipment. The jewel in the crown was Corning, which used the shell for a concert by the Boston Symphony on tour. Charles Munch conducted the event and spread the word among his colleagues that the shell provided orchestral balance, good onstage hearing, and a fine environment for symphonic presentation in the audience area.

That was the beginning of an eight-year run, during which we provided over forty symphonic shells to orchestras and theater owners throughout the United States. Among our clients were the New York Philharmonic, the Metropolitan Opera, the Detroit Symphony, the Cincinnati Symphony, the Los Angeles Philharmonic, the Pittsburgh Symphony, and lesser-known ensembles in Louisville, Fresno, Wheeling, and Atlanta. Theaters that acquired the shell included the Crampton Auditorium at Howard University, the Ravinia Music Festival, the Arie Crown Theater in Chicago, the Oakland Municipal Auditorium, in California, and the Brooklyn Academy of Music.

Designing and tuning so many of these shells gave me a unique opportunity to evaluate both audience area and stage acoustical environments. With the instrumentalists, repertory, and shells all being quite similar, the only acoustical variable was the room itself. This

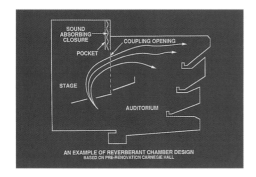

AN EXAMPLE OF REVERBERANT CHAMBER DESIGN
BASED ON PRE-RENOVATION CARNEGIE HALL

presented a unique opportunity for me to evaluate the environment of these spaces in regard to their geometry, seating arrangements, and materials of construction. In some instances, the quality of the sound was quite different than what the standard scientific literature of the day might have predicted.

One interesting phenomenon presented itself during the first installations. In addition to obtaining the positive results mentioned by Charles Munch, the shells were providing increased low-frequency reverberation that resulted in increased warmth. The light weight of the shell precluded the reflection of low-frequency energy, so how were we meeting this extremely important criterion with these light-weight units?

When I delivered a paper to the Acoustical Society of America in the early sixties providing data substantiating these results, several of my learned friends became very upset and called me a fakir and a charlatan. Luckily, some other colleagues took me to the bar, and two of them, Russell Johnson and Ted Schultz, suggested that the shell might be enabling a certain percentage of low-frequency energy to enter the stage house through the openings in the ceiling and that this energy, reverberating in the hard concrete and plaster stage house, was being returned to the stage platform and the listening area at extended lengths of time. This is an acoustical phenomenon known as acoustic coupling, which enables sound energy in a low absorptive space to couple back to a space with high absorption.

As I mentioned earlier, one of the main reasons we were able to couple sound successfully was that theater owners of that period rented their halls on a four-wall basis. When the symphonies moved in to set up these shells, there were no soft goods or scenery stored in the upper volume of these stage houses. To further reinforce this technique, we began to install sound-transparent curtains in place of the heavily absorptive main act curtains that had been used previously to block views of the rigging, light fixtures, and backstage

OPPOSITE: *Eugene McDermott Concert Hall, Morton H. Meyerson Symphony Center, Dallas, Texas. The first concert hall with tunable coupled chambers. Note the chamber doors in the ring just below the ceiling. Architect: Pei Cobb Freed and Partners. Acoustic and Theatre Planning: Artec Consultants Inc*

THE ACOUSTICS OF PERFORMANCE HALLS

walls. This seemed quite logical to me, and acoustic coupling techniques became a byword in all of my later designs for concert halls and music pavilions. Interestingly enough, Russell Johnson also found this technique useful, and starting with the construction of the McDermott Concert Hall in Dallas, he designed a number of coupled concert halls throughout the United States and Europe that proved to be outstandingly successful.

The Stagecraft shell refuted the perception that multipurpose halls were no-purpose halls. The architectural acoustician could develop an extremely satisfying symphonic acoustic environment for many multipurpose buildings that would come close to matching the symphonic acoustical characteristics of single-room concert halls and still enable the space to be used successfully for opera, ballet, Broadway musicals, and amplified popular concerts.

I felt the way Sean O'Casey described at the end of the first volume of his autobiography: "I learned poetry and had kissed a girl. If I hadn't gone to school, I had met the scholars; if I hadn't gone into the house, I had knocked at the door."

LESSONS LEARNED

COUPLED TUNABLE SYMPHONIC SHELLS

In an earlier chapter, I mentioned that many theater owners offer their facilities as a "four-wall rental," meaning that the stage deck and flies are bare and that the renter has the responsibility and the cost of loading scenery, shells, lighting, etc., in and out of the theater. Since the walls of these stage houses are made of concrete or brick, the hard walls of the space are very reverberant and lend themselves well to acoustic coupling techniques.

However, sometimes the theater owners permanently dress the stage with a full set of drapes and hang a number of strip lights on line sets at intervals required to facilitate an evenly lit stage (usually about 8 feet). They do this so they can rent the space for lectures and amplified popular concerts. Organizations and musical groups that sponsor these events usually don't own their own draperies, scenery, or lights and would find it too expensive to rent and install the equipment needed to mask the bare walls of the stage house and reduce reverberance for these performances. These drape sets comprise an upstage traveling curtain, side legs, and overhead teasers deployed to mask the stage walls, lights, and flies. Leaving these absorptive units in place once a demountable shell is installed will negate the coupling effect and create a dead rather than a live space surrounding the orchestra.

For this reason, it is necessary to eliminate the problem as quickly and economically as possible, since the orchestra might have rented the theater just for the day of the concert. It would be time-consuming and expensive to have to remove all the draperies from the line sets (the support pipes used to raise and lower the scenery) and reinstall them after the concert was over (probably having to pay stagehands overtime to accomplish these tasks). However, there is an alternate solution, and here is how you might handle the situation:

COUPLED TUNABLE SHELL INSTALLATION

1. Move the upstage traveling curtain offstage (gathered into the wings), flip the teasers (the cloth curtains suspended from the line sets) back on themselves on the line sets reducing their length by half, and gather and tie the legs with rope.
2. Once this is accomplished, go to the pin rail (the railing in the wings, used to raise and lower scenery) and take all the line sets on which these draperies are hung "out," or up, into the flies as far as they will go.

This in effect creates a reverse acoustic hard cap. The volume nearest the orchestra at deck level will be hard and reverberant throughout the mid and low portion of the frequency spectrum. In the listening area, as you will recall, "the hard cap" of the hall is at the top of the room. The lower part of the room, where the audience is seated, is more absorptive than the upper portion, allowing the reverberation to persist in time to the required length.

Since the tunable shell is designed with spaces between the ceiling units, in many instances it is possible to use the theater's existing strip lights as orchestra down lighting, eliminating the need to hang special lighting units for rehearsals and one or two performances.

Some points to note:

1. Strip light fixtures come in alternate colors of clear or straw, blue, and red. At the switchboard, one must kill the red and blue units, since they color the scores on the music stand a beautiful deep shade of purple, a phenomenon not truly appreciated by the musicians.

2. If the stage depth is too short and one finds after tuning the shell that the brass and percussion still overpower the strings, you might go to the pin rail and bring "in," or lower, the teaser located nearest the gap between the last ceiling and the rear wall of the shell. If this doesn't work, bring out the mutes and the muffled drumsticks or only program Mozart symphonies. (Just kidding.)

3. The first 5 or so feet (1.5 meters) of space directly behind the proscenium wall is a critical area for theatrical events. The line sets located in this area are needed for a main act curtain, main act teaser, a show curtain, a scrim curtain, and the first theatrical light pipe. In a four-wall rental other than the main act curtain and teaser, the line sets are empty and can be used to hang shell ceilings. However, the space between the first light pipe and the back of the proscenium arch is too narrow to accommodate a typical demountable shell ceiling unit (8 feet; 2.4 meters), and a special unit of approximately 4 feet can be

built and flown in that area in order to cover the violins and cellos located downstage near the lip of the performance platform.

4. With the main act curtain drawn offstage or flown out, the main act teaser will still be in place and will muffle a certain amount of coupled reverberation from the stage house. For optimum results, take "out" the main act teaser (lift it into the flies) and tie a sound-transparent scrim teaser on the line set directly behind the main act teaser to improve coupling capability. Select a light-colored scrim and gather it to some extent to avoid light bleeding through the material. Silkscreening a pattern on the scrim curtain will further mask the backstage area. (We designed such a scrim for Carnegie Hall when they installed the Rodgers electronic organ in the fly space of the stage house before the latest renovation).

Severance Hall

The renovation of Severance Hall was one of my most difficult assignments. If one is working on a new concert hall or renovating a facility that everyone acknowledges has defects, as long as the results are an improvement at all, success is assured. In the case of Severance Hall, we were informed that the main reason for the renovation on the stage platform was related to the symphony's desire to bring an unused organ, located in a sealed-off area of the flies, down to stage level. We were to redesign the acoustic shell to accommodate the instrument. In accomplishing this task, we were to maintain the exact acoustic environment of the space as it existed. There were to be no changes made to the architecture of the audience area and the footprint of the orchestra layout was to be as similar as possible to the existing area.

Bringing the organ to stage level meant designing a completely new physical stage enclosure that had to duplicate all reflective energy measurements onstage and in the audience area. To add to the difficulty, the existing shell was a contained structure with no tuning or coupling capabilities—the type of shell that is totally inflexible once installed. During an earlier renovation, this shell had been installed in the stage house of the original multiuse theater, which was built in 1930. In so doing, the designers acoustically sealed off the organ that had originally been located in the fly tower.

At the start of the design process, the musicians representing the orchestra on the building committee told us that their brethren had become used to the existing aural conditions onstage, felt comfortable in that environment, and were reluctant to consider any changes. However, at the first meeting of the design team with the full orchestra present, we were given a different evaluation by many members of the orchestra. They agreed with the assessments made in 1963 by a number of listeners that it was difficult to achieve orchestral balance between strings and brass and that the overall reverberation times were on the low side of admissible. In addition, and typical of a contained shell, the musicians had difficulty hearing one another.

This was good news for the acoustician. There were areas that needed improvement, and our client was looking to us to improve the aural environment for the orchestra and, as a result, the audience area as well. This meant the numbers could change within proper tolerances and our role was more than just a holding action. Of course, the fact that the musicians' acoustic committee threatened to hang me from the proscenium arch if anything went wrong kept me from being too exuberant.

Severance Hall, Cleveland, Ohio. View of original audience area. Architect: Walker & Weeks. Acoustics: Dayton C. Miller.

Severance Hall renovation, Cleveland, Ohio. Note the grille openings to coupled space on the side walls of the redesigned orchestra enclosure. Architect: David Schwartz. Acoustics: Jaffe Holden Scarbrough.

As one might have predicted on a project of this scale, I was handed another curve ball. The executive director of the Cleveland Orchestra, Tom Morris, was distrustful of tunable, coupled orchestra shells and insisted that we have a permanent, nontunable ceiling. I tried to persuade him otherwise, by referring to our many successful projects utilizing this technique. But he was adamant. Therefore, I looked for a way of modifying my technique in such a way that I would still come up with successful results.

To accomplish this, I designed a fixed ceiling with permanent openings to the reverberant stage house and a partial open back wall, incorporating faux organ pipes and a number of reverberant chambers coupled to the side walls of the shell towers. The chambers, the ceiling openings, and the faux organ pipes provided me with opportunities to couple the original stage house of the 1930 design, and the variability of the grille openings gave me a number of tuning capabilities.

Severance Hall renovation, Cleveland, Ohio. The design of the new orchestra enclosure blends with the architectural design of the hall. Architect: David Schwartz. Acoustics: Jaffe Holden Scarbrough.

This design direction was approved by all concerned during the schematic design phase, and David Schwarz, the architect, and I implemented all of these elements as the design progressed.

The flexibility of the coupling approach was somewhat reduced because the large low-frequency organ pipes had to be positioned within the coupled chambers. However, the renovation was an architectural and acoustic success, Janelle Gelfand, music critic of the *Cincinnati Enquirer*, wrote: "It is the most visually stunning setting for an orchestra this side of Vienna's Musikverein. Even better, its pristine acoustics—the quality responsible for the Cleveland Sound—have been preserved and even slightly enhanced." Thus, much to my relief, the musicians were denied the pleasure of a necktie party featuring the guy they called the "sound man."

TEN

SYMPHONIC SUMMER
MUSIC PAVILLIONS

Just as the symphonic scene dominates winter music in the United States, so it does during the summer festivals. Most major orchestras are tied up with festivals in their summer homes.

—Harold Schonberg

The development of symphonic summer music pavilions has been a distinctly American phenomenon. These pavilions were an outgrowth of the Chautauqua Methodist Assembly on Chautauqua Lake in far western New York. Founded in 1874 as a vacation and learning camp for Sunday school teachers, it developed into an ecumenical retreat offering courses in academic studies, art, and music. In 1920, the Chautauqua Symphony Orchestra was formed to create one of the first outdoor symphonic summer music festivals. Concerts were held in a 5,000-seat indoor-outdoor music shed. The results were gratifying, and the Methodists opened camps in different states to create a circuit of lectures and concerts in other venues. This organization actually predated the Schubert and the Keith-Orpheum companies in creating touring circuits.

The concept of the music festival expanded in the 1930s when the Boston Symphony, the New York Philharmonic, and the Los Angeles Philharmonic began to present al fresco concerts. The

Boston Symphony Orchestra started a summer music festival at the Dan Hanna Farm horse ring in the Berkshire Mountains of Massachusetts, which became the Tanglewood Music Festival. The New York Philharmonic began a series of summer concerts at Lewisohn Stadium on the campus of the City College of New York, and the Los Angeles Philharmonic began performing at the Hollywood Bowl.

Lewisohn Stadium and the Hollywood Bowl are open-air amphitheaters with the orchestras enclosed in shell-like structures, while the Chautauqua and Tanglewood musicians performed in fan-shaped wooden pavilions with side walls open to a vast expanse of lawn. Although the lawn areas of the pavilion concerts were eventually reinforced with sound systems, initially the sheds relied on the natural acoustic environments under the roof structures. The quality of orchestral sound in these sheds was considered quite acceptable thanks to the large volume of air under the pavilion roof in relation to the relatively low absorption characteristics of people seated on hard camp or folding chairs. This condition provided reverberation times at mid and low frequencies that were comparable to those found in the shoebox-style European halls and resulted in a live and warm aural envelope. The only thing missing from the sound quality was a certain amount of presence and clarity, since the open side walls could not furnish the early reflected energy necessary for these important musical characteristics.

In the 1950s, the Boston Symphony asked the acoustical firm of Bolt, Beranek & Newman to assist them in improving musical presence at the Tanglewood shed. BB&N installed a series of reflectors designed by Eero Saarinen over the orchestra and a third of the audience members. The overhead reflectors provided the proper early reflections on stage and throughout the seating area and brought the quality of the symphonic environment up to par with some of the best indoor concert halls.

Serious outdoor symphonic programming has been firmly established as part of the cultural and social fabric of American music. In the past, some noted music directors refused to conduct pavilion concerts because they believed the resultant sound would be below their standards. Leonard Bernstein opted out of the first New York Philharmonic Central Park concert in 1965. However, when 60,000 people showed up for that event, he had a change of heart and was on the podium the following year leading the band as usual. Whether one is for or against moving the classical repertoire of the symphony orchestra out of the concert hall and into the fresh air, there is a noticeable trend in this direction.

Outdoor classical performances by major symphonies fall into three basic categories. The most sophisticated is the five- or six-week summer festival run in conjunction with a professional-level music school. The Boston Symphony's complex at Tanglewood in Lenox, Massachusetts, and the Ravinia Festival in Highland Park, Illinois, featuring the Chicago Symphony, are the best examples of this type of operation. In both instances, concerts are given in a shedlike structure with an acoustic environment designed specifically for orchestral performance. These pavilions have no balconies, and the hard, boxlike upper roof provides the required symphonic reverberation times. The lower side and rear walls are open to the lawn area at a height of about 18 feet (5.5 meters). Presence and intimacy are provided by canopy systems that cover the stage and a portion of the audience.

The second category is identical to the first, except that the facilities are not affiliated with a major music education program. Orchestral concerts at the Robin Hood Dell in Philadelphia, the Saratoga Performing Arts Center in Saratoga Springs, New York, and Wolf Trap Farm Park in Vienna, Virginia, are representative of this form of activity.

The third type of outdoor performance is an orchestra in front

Marjorie Merriweather Post Pavilion, Columbia, Maryland. Roof configuration develops indoor concert hall environment. Architect: Gehry Walsh and O'Malley. Acoustics: Christopher Jaffe.

THE ACOUSTICS OF PERFORMANCE HALLS

of a large audience in an amphitheater setting or on a vast expanse of park lawn. The Los Angeles Philharmonic concerts at the Hollywood Bowl, the Boston Pops Orchestra at the Hatch Shell on the Boston Esplanade, and the New York Philharmonic concerts at the Carlos Moseley Pavilion in Central Park are examples of this form of presentation and are discussed in the next chapter.

When symphony orchestras first thought in terms of outdoor summer music programs, little consideration was given to the acoustic quality of the various venues in which they performed. It was taken for granted that al fresco concerts would never deliver the traditional sound of the best indoor halls. However, as acousticians learned more about the relationships between subjective listening quality and the measurements of reflected energy, many of these pavilions were renovated to provide the acoustic characteristics of indoor concert facilities.

In July of 1967, at the opening of the Merriweather Post Pavilion in Columbia, Maryland (initially the summer home of the Washington National Symphony), Harold Schonberg of the *New York Times* wrote: "Even at the rehearsal, and this was confirmed the following night, it was clear that Jaffe and his associates had come up with probably the best-sounding outdoor hall in the United States. It may be hard to believe, but the Merriweather Post Pavilion of Music is better than most regulation indoor concert halls."

Outdoor concerts have the potential advantage of relaxed behavior restrictions and pleasant environmental settings. On the other hand, concerts performed without a pavilion covering the audience can be problematic. Without a shed or cover to contain sound energy, high and low frequencies will dissipate as the distance from the stage increases, resulting in a flat, mid-range sound similar to a cheap car radio. In addition, one has to be careful of the location of all outdoor symphonic events and select quiet environments relatively free of airplane, highway, and mechanical-system noise. Both the audience and the musicians can be bothered by hot, humid days or nights, and wind can blow the players' parts off the music stands.

(Large wooden clothespins are sometimes used avoid this.) For all of these reasons, and the fact that only financially sound orchestras could afford to schedule a summer season, very few major American orchestras attempted to build sheds and produce summer music festivals. Then the Ford Foundation came to the rescue.

In the first half of the twentieth century, symphony musicians were contracted to play for only two-thirds of the year because of the lack of proper air-conditioning in traditional halls. Players had to find additional sources of income over the summer months. Some worked in popular music and movie recording studios, while others hoped to find work in summer resorts and at weddings. Salaries at all but the ten or so major orchestras were extremely low throughout this period. In the early 1960s, the Atlanta Symphony offered a starting salary of $4,000 a year and an opportunity to teach music in the local school system as an added benefit. The last chair in the second violin section of this same orchestra earned extra money as the head stage hand and drove the symphony truck during statewide tours.

In order to relieve this condition and stabilize the life of professional symphony musicians, the Ford Foundation gave matching grants to all the major and several of the intermediate-sized orchestras in America so that they could offer musicians a fifty-two-week employment contract. These generous grants resulted in the development of twenty or more summer festivals during the sixties and seventies. Symphony management reasoned that as long as they were paying musicians a salary over the summer months, they should put them to work in a music festival and recoup some of that money. They would have to raise money for the physical facilities; however, it is always easier to get donor gifts for a building than for mundane operating expenses such as musicians' salaries.

The first organization to opt for a festival after the announcement of the Ford Foundation grants was the Detroit Symphony, which, partnering with Oakland University in Rochester, Michigan, selected a site at the former estate of Matilda Dodge Wilson that had been donated to the university. Soon to follow were festivals by the Philadelphia Orchestra, the Washington National Symphony, the New York Philharmonic, the Metropolitan Opera, the Cleveland Orchestra, the Saint Louis Symphony, and the Cincinnati Symphony. During this period, both the Los Angeles Philharmonic and the Chicago Symphony upgraded their existing facilities, and all but the Metropolitan Opera, the New York Philharmonic, and the Los Angeles Philharmonic opted to perform in partially enclosed, shed-like music pavilions.

In the fall of 1963, I designed a portable shell and sound system for an outdoor concert by the New York Philharmonic at the Monterey County Fairgrounds in California. The musicians were extremely pleased with the acoustical environment of the shell, and Carlos Moseley, executive director of the Philharmonic, recommended me to his colleagues at the Detroit Symphony, who at that time were planning to establish a major music festival in Michigan and were looking for an acoustician to assist them in designing a symphonic pavilion. During this period, the firm of Bolt, Beranek & Newman was the high-profile star of the acoustic consulting profession and

Riverbend Music Pavilion, Cincinnati, Ohio. The pergola behind the lawn seating adds reverberation for listeners in that location. Architect: Michael Graves and Associates. Acoustics: Jaffe Acoustics.

Howard C. Baldwin Memorial Pavilion at Meadowbrook, Oakland University, Rochester, Michigan. RIGHT: *Stagehouse coupling provides concert hall reverberation.* BELOW: *An extensive canopy system forward of the proscenium compensates for lack of side walls. Architect: O'Dell Hewlett & Luckenbach. Acoustics: Christopher Jaffe.*

had received kudos for its work at Tanglewood. However, based on Moseley's recommendation, they hired me.

Until then, my experience had been exclusively with designing acoustic shells for orchestras. This was to be my first building project, and I was as nervous as Maggie the cat on a hot tin roof. Since tunable coupled shells were responsible for my success to date, I decided to follow the same approach that had worked so well for orchestras performing with these shells in vaudeville theaters, movie houses, and multiuse theaters. In other words, I would surround the stage platform with a 200,000-cubic-foot (5,663-cubic-meter) structure and place a tunable coupled shell within it. For the audience area, I would use the Tanglewood shed acoustic criteria as a guide to selecting the volume-to-audience absorption ratio.

The resulting Baldwin Pavilion at the Meadow Brook Music Festival was set in a steep ravine with dense woods on either side of the building. The facility accommodated 2,200 people under the shed roof with a lawn area for another 2,000. We constructed the stage house and placed the tunable coupled shell within it. Since there were no side walls, we extended a forestage canopy 25 feet (7.6 meters) forward of the stage platform to provide early reflections to audience members. We designed the audience area of the shed with a volume of 660,000 cubic feet (18,689 cubic meters), or 300 cubic feet (8.5 cubic meters) per person seated under the roof. The results were very gratifying. After the opening concert, Irving Lowens of the *Washington Star* commented: "The Howard C. Baldwin Pavilion is much more than handsome—it is an astonishingly successful acoustic achievement. It focuses orchestral sound with amazing clarity. Indeed there are few indoor concert halls to match it."

This was the start of my career as a concert hall acoustician. The success of Meadow Brook convinced the musical community of the effectiveness of this design approach, and over the next ten years I received commissions to design music pavilions for the Washington National Symphony, the Cleveland Orchestra, the Saint Louis Symphony, the Chicago Symphony, the Toronto Symphony, the San

Francisco Symphony, and the Cincinnati Symphony, as well as to redesign the amphitheaters at Lewisohn Stadium and the Hollywood Bowl and to create a touring stage and shell for the New York Philharmonic parks concerts.

The plans and sections of these buildings illustrate the similarity of the acoustic design used to produce the required qualities of liveness, clarity, and warmth. The Forum at Ontario Place and the Concord Pavilion, designed as summer homes for the Toronto and San Francisco symphonies respectively, broke away from the end stage model and were developed as surround concert pavilions.

It is interesting to note that all of these pavilions coupled sound in different architectural geometries, even though the roof lines of the buildings are dramatically different. Meadow Brook, Merriweather Post, and Cincinnati's Riverbend Music Center integrate stage-house and audience volume, while the Cleveland Orchestra's Blossom Music Center accomplished this feat in a backstage area open to the hall behind the acoustical shell. The Mississippi River Festival facility, summer home of the Saint Louis Symphony, coupled space in a steel enclosure surrounding the stage platform, and the Concord Pavilion outside San Francisco used a moat under the stage for the coupling effect. Some pavilion roofs were flat and some were angled. Blossom Center has a conical roof and the Saint Louis Symphony performed in an oval circus tent, as mentioned above. Both the Toronto pavilion and the Concord Pavilion were surround-style facilities but they had totally different roof lines.

Since the side and rear walls of a music pavilion are open to a height of approximately18 feet (5.5 meters) to 20 feet (6 meters), reverberation from the coupled space of the stage house becomes a key element in the design process. An added improvement of these latter-day pavilions was the fact that the audience was seated on a 10- to 12-degree slope, compared to Tanglewood and Chautauqua, which have flat seating areas in the pavilions and on the lawns as well. I note these differences to reemphasize that it is the reflecting patterns that provide the traditional symphonic sound and not

Saint Louis Symphony, Mississippi River Festival Pavilion, Southern Illinois University, Edwardsville, Illinois. ABOVE: *Note the forestage reflectors providing intimacy and clarity in this fan-shaped hall.* LEFT: *Steel box surrounding the orchestra enclosure provides needed reverberation. Architect: Anselevicius, Rupe, and Medlin. Acoustics: Jaffe Acoustics.*

Ontario Place Pavilion, Toronto, Canada. Opening day at surround-style symphonic music pavilion. Architect: Zeidler Partnership. Acoustics: Jaffe Acoustics, Inc.

specific architectural styles, such as the shoebox design of the Vienna and Boston halls. Copy the reflecting patterns, not the architectural forms.

Modeled after Chautauqua and Tanglewood, all of these festivals incorporated a large lawn area for those who like to sit under the stars with a picnic basket and a bottle of Pinot Noir. The lawns at Blossom Center and Ravinia could accommodate 10,000 to 15,000 people, and some form of sound reinforcement was necessary to provide a satisfactory listening experience. However, the lawn area at Meadow Brook was small and the rake was quite steep, making it unnecessary to amplify sound for those outside the pavilion. It was at the back of the lawn at Meadow Brook that Wally Collins, dean of the music school at Oakland University, discovered that as good as the sound was on the lawn, it was even better if you donned a pair of Mickey Mouse ears.

As mentioned earlier, there can be hazards as well as rewards in performing outdoors. Depending on the location, there are problems in physically bringing the musicians and their instruments to the sites. On opening night at the Mississippi River Festival on the

Ravinia Music Festival, Highland Park, Illinois. Lawn seating at the Ravinia Festival. Architect: Holabird and Root. Acoustics: Jaffe Acoustics, Inc.

Edwardsville Campus of the University of Illinois, the conductor of the Saint Louis Symphony forgot his dress pants and Peter Pastreich, the executive director, had to lend him his pair to mount the podium on time. Then Peter had to drive back to Saint Louis to obtain a new pair for himself so he could attend the postconcert reception. It pays to have a conductor and an executive director with the same waist size, although a conductor in tails and undershorts might have started an important new fashion trend in the symphonic world.

Symphony management can be plagued with other nonmusical problems in producing al fresco concerts, among them inadequate stage lighting and limited toilet and dressing facilities. The large lawn presentations lessen visual intimacy, and immense audiences require strict security and crowd control.

However, there is no question that the rewards that accompany such efforts outweigh the hazards. These concerts place the symphony in the front lines of cultural enhancement programs that enrich many lives and help remedy cultural deprivation. Such programming increases exposure and builds up audiences for the indoor concert season. Aside from the orchestra, the community benefits

The Blossom Music Center, Cayahuga Falls, Ohio. Lawn audiences enjoying a Cleveland Orchestra concert. Architect: Schafer, Flynn & van Dijk. Acoustics: Christopher Jaffe.

through the development of a more sophisticated and culturally aware public. The benefit to the musicians of full-year employment is an important factor in increasing the dignity of the musical profession and will enable more instrumentalists and conductors to follow a lifelong career.

Blossom Music Center

In the fall of 1966, after the successful openings of the Meadow Brook's Baldwin Pavilion for the Detroit Symphony and the Merriweather Post Pavilion for the Washington National Symphony, I received a conference call from Beverly Barksdale and George Szell, the executive director and the music director of the Cleveland Orchestra.

They were well aware of the fine reception these pavilions had received from the musical community and invited me to act as the acoustician for a new summer home for the Cleveland Orchestra in Northampton Township, a sylvan area near the Cuyahoga River midway between Cleveland and Akron.

Peter van Dijk, a talented young designer who had worked for many years at the Saarinen firm in Hamden, Connecticut, was selected as the architect, and it was decided that he, Mr. Barksdale, and I would tour a number of existing music pavilions before settling down to the design process.

The first pavilion we visited was the Tanglewood facility, a one-level fan-shaped building. Although the sound was quite good, none of us believed that the design of the plain, pie-shaped shed would meet the architectural design expectations of the Cleveland community. The next day, we left for Saratoga Springs, where Arnold Vollmer had just designed the Saratoga Performing Arts Center, a new multiuse pavilion for the Philadelphia Orchestra and the New York City Ballet and Opera companies. This building had a balcony to bring audiences closer to the stage for theatrical events and a steeply raked orchestra floor for improved sightlines. The facility had been open for only a year or so but was already noted for accommodating the needs of the conductor of the orchestra, Eugene Ormandy. Although the musicians had to suffer through the humid Saratoga summer heat, a special air-conditioned podium was built for the maestro. In addition, a creek that ran near the pavilion and bubbled too loudly was dammed at Ormandy's request. Nothing could really be done about the crickets.

After attending a concert of the Philadelphia Orchestra at the pavilion, the three of us had a late dinner at a Lake George restaurant a short distance from the festival site. We began to discuss the plans for the Cleveland building, and Peter van Dijk asked me

The Blossom Music Center, Cayahuga Falls, Ohio. The conical roof line provides indoor-like reverberation. Architect: Schafer, Flynn & Van Dijk. Acoustics: Christopher Jaffe.

where one should sit to hear the finest orchestral sound in the best-loved concert halls around the world. I replied that the best-liked orchestral sound could always be found in the upper balconies of these halls and suggested that perhaps we should design the new pavilion for the Cleveland Orchestra as the world's biggest balcony.

At first we all laughed at the thought, but as the evening wore on and the idea took shape, Pete and I sketched out a design on the back of a napkin. That sketch evolved into the final design of the facility, and Blossom Music Center stands today as a fine al fresco music pavilion and as the world's biggest balcony.

I developed the acoustic design of the pavilion on the basis of the acoustic criteria I had used for indoor multiuse halls and the earlier pavilions. I set the air volume at 300 cubic feet per person, a total of 1,500,000 cubic feet (42,475 cubic meters) for an audience of 5,000 people, and counted on a sloping roof and an extensive canopy system over the orchestra and one-third of the audience for the early reflections that were needed to supply intimacy and clarity for the audience and onstage hearing capability for the musicians. Since low frequencies are not absorbed by air, I knew we would develop a good bass ratio for warmth with such a large air volume.

The unique thing about the design was the placement of the orchestra platform and shell-like sound walls forward of the open backstage area, and the use of the air volume at the rear of the pavilion. The results speak for themselves. The pavilion opened to wide acclaim and became the home to one of America's most prestigious orchestral festivals.

George Szell, the conductor of the Cleveland Orchestra at that time, was known to be a martinet on the order of Toscanini. On opening night, toward the end of the first half of the program, a loud bang reverberated through the pavilion. I thought a stagehand had dropped a hammer behind the shell and feared for the fellow's life as well as for mine, since I had designed an open backstage area. All remained quiet at intermission, but during the second half of the concert—Bang!—another loud crash.

Pete and I were stupefied. We were proud to have designed and built what we felt was an architecturally beautiful and acoustically fine facility, and now mysterious noises were spoiling the concerts. As the season progressed, the sounds were traced to the steel in the building structure, and sensors were placed on all of the beams and trusses. When the data were analyzed, the mystery was solved. Workmen had neglected to file off the burrs on a number of strain-relief slots, and as the early evening temperatures dropped, some of the steel members became caught on the burrs. When the strain became too great, the steel slipped over the burrs and banged down onto the base of the slots. A few walks on the high steel with a power tool, and the noises disappeared. A happy ending after all.

ELEVEN

AMPHITHEATERS AND MOBILE SYMPHONY STAGES

They started arriving at 10 o'clock in the morning yesterday, just about the time the orchestra began rehearsing. They laid their blankets on the ground to keep their places. By 7:30 in the evening, the Sheep Meadow in Central Park was a sea of people who had come to hear the New York Philharmonic's opening program in its 11th season of free concerts in the city's parks.

—Raymond Ericson

DON'T FENCE ME IN

While some orchestras choose to present their summer festivals in indoor-outdoor music pavilions, others present their offerings in amphitheaters or, in the case of the New York Philharmonic and the Boston Pops Orchestra, on lawns in Central Park and the Esplanade on the Charles River. The amphitheater used by the Los Angeles Philharmonic, which charges admission for festival events, seats 18,000 people. The New York Philharmonic and Boston Pops concerts are free performances; crowds of over 100,000 people have been recorded at the Sheep Meadow (the original venue) and the Great Lawn in Central Park, where the outdoor concerts of the Philharmonic and the Metropolitan Opera are now held.

An amphitheater has no roof over the audience seating area, and the source area varies from location to location. At Lewisohn

Lewisohn Stadium, CUNY, New York, N.Y. Metropolitan Opera Series of summer concerts, 1965 and 1966. Shell and sound system designer: Christopher Jaffe.

Stadium on the campus of the City College of New York in upper Manhattan, where the Metropolitan Opera performed in 1965 and 1966, the source area was a 5,000-square-foot (465-square-meter) stage with a 40-foot (12-meter)-high concrete fly space and a proscenium opening of 100 feet (30 meters). Velour draperies positioned left and right of the orchestra shell created a modest set of wings in which the musicians and choristers could gather. At the rear of the stadium, behind the stepped concrete amphitheater seating, a concrete pergola provided a natural, resonant sound to listeners in that location.

I designed the source area for the Met Orchestra using my tried-and-true approach. A tunable acoustical shell of fiberglass-reinforced polyester was positioned within the 200,000-cubic-foot (5,663-cubic-meter) volume of the hard concrete stage house. The acoustic characteristics of this arrangement provided the musicians and those seated near the front of the stage with a live, warm, and clear natural sound.

In order to provide those patrons farthest from the stage with the best possible reinforced sound, we specified column loudspeakers built by Rudy Bozak's firm in Norwalk, Connecticut, as the heart of the amplification system. These units were supplemented with infinite-baffle bass loudspeakers and had the lowest harmonic distortion of any manufacturer's product available at the time. The column speakers had the added advantage of providing an extremely even distribution of sound energy over the vast reaches of the stadium.

We had had great success with comparable speakers several years earlier at a series of youth concerts presented by Jacqueline Kennedy on the White House lawn as well as at a performance of the Philadelphia Orchestra at the Garden State Racetrack in New Jersey. These speakers were a key element in the success of the concerts presented at Lewisohn Stadium, the Hollywood Bowl, and Central Park. The only alternative to the Bozak speakers would have been the harsh horn speakers used for outdoor public address systems that had led so many musicians and audience members to dislike and avoid amplified outdoor symphonic concerts.

The Lewisohn Stadium concerts were well received by the *New York Times* and the administrative staff of the Metropolitan Opera Company. Charles Riecker, the artist coordinator for the Met and one of the project managers for the stadium series, was extremely impressed by the sound. Listening to Licia Albanese while standing with me in the pergola, Mr. Riecker commented, "She has such a soft voice, I was worried it would be lost in the vast spaces of this facility. I can hear that beautiful voice as clearly as if we were seated in the opera house itself."

A very different and even more difficult assignment came to me with the opportunity to work with the Los Angeles Philharmonic on the renovation of the Hollywood Bowl amphitheater in 1970. The source area of this facility was the elliptical bowl-shaped structure made famous throughout the country in newspaper reports and motion pictures; some people even remembered Oscar Levant playing Gershwin's *Rhapsody in Blue* at the Bowl in the film of that name in 1945. Working at the bowl was, in fact, working in the fishbowl that is the Los Angeles film and recording industries.

The main symphonic acoustic problem with the facility was the elliptically shaped bowl, which inappropriately focused the sound of individual instruments of the orchestra during passages for full orchestra. In the middle of a Beethoven symphony, a clarinet would suddenly come through with such power that you might think you were listening to a Mozart clarinet concerto. William Severence, executive director of the Bowl, realized this shortcoming and sprayed the entire interior surface of the structure with an absorptive acoustic material. This eliminated the focusing but produced a dead acoustic space around the musicians, creating what might be described as the largest hi-fi set in the world. The only sound heard by audiences at the Bowl was coming through electronically amplified speakers. Big, ugly horn speakers, no less.

My solution was to remove the acoustical fuzz and insert a coupled tunable shell within the volume of the more reverberant space. This was the same approach we had been using for vaudeville houses, music pavilions, and the amphitheater at Lewisohn Stadium, but for the Bowl, the inner shell was a unique design that I developed in conjunction with the architect Frank Gehry. At the time, Frank was designing chairs and tables out of the same cardboard used to make laundry boxes, and he asked me if I could design a symphonic shell made from this material. As you know, an orchestra shell has to have some stiffness and weight to be effective, and cardboard box material really wouldn't do.

However, Frank Gehry always challenged me to exert my last ounce of creativity, and I suggested that we might consider fabricating the shell out of the tubular cardboard forms used to create the concrete columns that support interchanges on expressways. The many layers of cardboard used to fabricate these forms result in a hard reflective surface and the tubular form adds to its stiffness. We built both the side towers and the ceilings out of these tubes. For good measure, I decided to use the tubes to create a cardboard organ.

Hollywood Bowl, Los Angeles, California. TOP: *Nighttime view of concert enclosure with cardboard turntable tubes for the Los Angeles Philharmonic.* LEFT: *Daytime view of concert enclosure. Architect: Frank O. Gehry. Acoustics: Jaffe Acoustics.*

I tuned each tube to a particular frequency and dampened the cavities by filling them with fiberglass insulation material. This had the effect of spreading the frequency characteristics of the individual pipes. Without the fiberglass, each tube would have resonated at a single note and we would have gone back to old clarinet problem again. Frank Gehry and I are joint patent holders on tubular cardboard acoustic concert enclosures.

To provide amplified sound to the large audiences at the Bowl, we turned once again to the Bozak column speakers as part of the sound-system design.

We did encounter one problem at the Bowl as the season progressed. The speakers located at the front of the stage, when adjusted to create the most natural sound in the box seats directly in front of the stage, did not provide enough volume at the rear of the seating area. We had to increase the percentage of amplified sound to the mix and lost some of the early "magic" of opening night. Lewisohn Stadium had one acoustic advantage over the Bowl in this regard. The concrete pergola surrounding the stepped seating banks at the rear of the facility allowed sound entering the pergola to develop a natural reverberation, which added to the aural fullness and presence for those seated on the steps. For that reason, we did not have to push the levels of the sound system as high as we did at the Bowl.

BEACH BLANKET BINGO

A music pavilion and even an amphitheater with a stage structure allows the acoustician to provide excellent sound to large audiences, but how does one approach a lawn concert when the local parks department restricts any form of permanent building and won't even let you smooth the ground for a temporary stage?

The New York Philharmonic park concert series, an example of the free lawn performance, was faced with these problems. The series was conceived by Carlos Moseley, the executive director of the Philharmonic, who decided it was imperative that his orchestra stay in New York City and present concerts for the local populace rather than seek out a sylvan site in the mountains and produce a music festival for vacationers and weekend travelers. With the Ford Foundation money covering operational costs, he tapped the National Endowment for the Arts, New York City, New York State, corporations, local foundations, and private donors to present the New York Philharmonic Concerts in the Parks, a three-week tour of the Philharmonic through the five boroughs of the city. There would be three concert programs, and each concert would be repeated in each borough throughout the week.

The problem, of course, was how to move a concert stage with a sound system designed to handle 10,000 people, accommodations for 95 musicians, a chorus of 100, dressing rooms for the conductor and soloists, portable generators, and restroom facilities for the audience from borough to borough within a twelve-hour period so that the facility would be up and running at 8 p.m. for the next evening's concert.

In the spring of 1963, Moseley invited me to his office at Lincoln Center to discuss the viability of his idea for this innovative festival. The idea was bold and challenging. Nothing like this had ever been done before, and we agreed that the first step must be for my firm, together with a representative of the orchestra, to conduct a feasibility study, selecting appropriate sites and sketching a preliminary design for a touring concert stage. Albert Knickerbocker (Nick) Webster was the assistant manager of the orchestra at the time, and he and I proceeded to check out sites and discuss design possibilities with structural engineers and truck body fabricators. Trailerized homes and portable lavatories had been built in the past, and we talked with manufacturers to determine if such devices could be adapted for our purposes (and at what cost). A key player in this operation was Peter Feller, the well-known Broadway set builder, who, using his theatrical tricks, came up with ways to fold the ceilings and floors of the stage to form a truck body and showed us how to pack a concert shell and other equipment within the trailers themselves.

Nick and I went back to the Philharmonic with a positive report. We found that it *was* feasible to build such a device in the form of four

The Minnie Guggenheimer
Touring Concert stage and
shell, New York, New York.
ABOVE: *Stage setup at Sheep
Meadow in Central Park.*
RIGHT: *Stage hands setting
ceiling units of acoustic
enclosure. Project designer:
Christopher Jaffe. Acoustics:
Christopher Jaffe.*

THE ACOUSTICS OF PERFORMANCE HALLS

interconnected trailers that could be moved from park to park by standard tractors. However, this was just the start of a long and difficult journey through the bureaucracy of a major metropolitan city.

The New York City Buildings Department insisted that we obtain a regular building permit for the trailers in every borough of the city and couldn't understand why we wanted a wooden rather than a steel floor under the orchestra. I had told the Philharmonic that a steel floor would destroy the sound quality of the orchestra, and Moseley asked Newbold Morris, then parks commissioner, to call his counterpart in the Buildings Department and insist on a wooden floor. The buildings commissioner argued that the safety of the public was at risk with a wooden floor, that building codes called for steel, and that this facility was ruled a building. Morris responded by saying that the public would never be near the structure. In fact, if anything happened, the only people affected by a shell collapse would be the musicians. Carlos Moseley and I were sitting next to Commissioner Morris when he made that statement, and Carlos turned a whiter shade of pale. Of course, we could have designed an ejection podium for Maestro Bernstein in an emergency.

The Minnie Guggenheimer Touring Concert stage and shell, New York City, New York. Erection of main structural trusses. Project designer: Christopher Jaffe. Acoustics: Christopher Jaffe.

Then the Parks Department stepped in with their rules and regulations. Yes, we could use the parks for concerts, but we would not be permitted to level the ground for the four trailer beds or run underground audio cables. (We almost lost the first concert in Brooklyn's Prospect Park because of uneven ground.) Finally, they allowed us to level the ground for the trailers and we encountered no further problems during the tour.

My firm, Stagecraft Corporation, acted as the acoustic and theater consultant for the project as well as the general contractor. Although the program for the trailers was developed by the Philharmonic, our contracts were with the City of New York. Between the bureaucracies of the Buildings and Parks departments and other internal departmental squabbles, it's a miracle that we finally got it done.

Working with my associates Peter Quaintance, Peter Feller, and Nick Webster on the physical facility and with Rudy Bozak on the sound, we opened the festival on the Sheep Meadow in Central Park in early August of 1965. The facility was named the Minnie Guggenheimer Stage and Shell in honor of the woman who sponsored those early concerts by the Philharmonic at Lewisohn Stadium in the 1930s.

Carlos Moseley had told me to design the sound system for 10,000 people. An audience of 60,000 showed up. I will admit that the sound was a little thin in the far reaches of the lawn; the response, however, was overwhelming. We moved the stage and shell to Prospect Park for a concert the next night and then on to Crocheron Park in Queens, the New York Botanical Garden in the Bronx, and finally, Silver Lake Park on Staten Island.

Dr. William Steinberg, the conductor of the Pittsburgh Symphony, had been brought in to do the honors for the entire festival tour. That first week, in Crocheron Park, we were faced with threatening weather. The opening-week concert was Beethoven's Ninth Symphony and Carlos Moseley did not want the audience to miss hearing the fourth movement with its great choral "Ode to Joy." He asked Dr. Steinberg if it would be all right to start the symphony with the fourth movement. Dr. Steinberg agreed and history was made. In the hundred-plus years of the New York Philharmonic, this was the only time it opened Beethoven's Ninth with the last movement. The orchestra did not get to play the entire work before the deluge came down, but the audience did get to hear the most thrilling part of the work.

How did I design the shell? There was no opportunity to create a coupled space with tunable reflectors within the dimensions of the trailers, and since the musicians were not keen on getting wet, I had to build a solid shell roof, just the kind of design that was against my religion. What to do?

Since a key task for a shell is to balance and blend the sections of the orchestra, I cut off the top of the rear shell panels to allow

The Minnie Guggenheimer Touring Concert stage and shell at Daffodil Hill, Bronx Botanical Gardens, New York. Project designer: Christopher Jaffe. Acoustics: Christopher Jaffe.

some of the high-energy brass and percussion energy to dissipate, and patched in some absorptive material in the ceiling to improve blend and prevent the sound from getting too harsh and loud on stage. These elements also enabled the musicians to hear themselves and other sections of the ensemble.

For the missing "coupled reverberation," I integrated a Philips four-output tape loop signal delay in the audio circuit. This device records the musical program and reproduces the signal at four different time intervals. This gave the audience a sense of a reverberant field. Not as effective as what we do today, but considered a milestone at the time.

In 1967, the Metropolitan Opera began presenting in a series of concert versions of operas using the same facility. Although the Lewisohn Stadium concerts had been a success the first year, the lack of

Carlos Mosley Pavilion, New York City, New York. Stage and shell erected at great lawn in Central Park. Project Designer: Peter Wexler; Architect: FTL Associates. Acoustics: Jaffe Holden Scarbrough.

THE ACOUSTICS OF PERFORMANCE HALLS

parking and a sense that the neighborhood had become somewhat dangerous dampened the enthusiasm of audiences the second year.

Because I had no idea the opera would be using the "Minnie" trailers when I designed the units, the Metropolitan orchestra and choristers were somewhat squeezed together for these presentations, which made it difficult to find optimum microphone placements for the best sound mix. One evening, I was standing at the rear of the crowd at Central Park with Rudolf Bing, director of the Met and a man known to be quite free in his criticism of shoddy work. I mentioned to him the problem associated with the small area of the shell for Met performances and hoped he was satisfied with the orchestral sound. He replied, "Forget the orchestra . . . just make sure we hear the singers."

Speaking of the singers, we had our hands full with that group.

Carlos Mosley Pavilion, New York City, New York. Signal-delayed distributed portable loudspeaker system. Sound system designers: David Robb/Christopher Jaffe.

They were all positioned on the apron of the stage, forward of the orchestra—each with his or her own microphone. Opera singers have tremendous vocal energy and should stand back at some distance from the microphone in performance. However, this was not their style. No matter what we told them, as the concert progressed, each one kept creeping closer and closer to the mikes. If one of them saw a colleague inching up, you can be sure he or she was on the move in a few minutes. We tried moving the microphones as close as possible to the stage lip, but it didn't help. finally, I hit on a solution. I positioned several wardrobe trunks on the grass in front of the stage and placed the mikes on the trunks. Any singer who got too close to the mike would fall off the stage. Voilà—it worked.

The parks concerts of the Philharmonic and the Met have become part of the cultural heritage of New York City. After forty-three years, they are still being presented every summer. All New Yorkers are indebted to Carlos Moseley, the man who came up with the idea and guided it to fruition.

TWELVE

CONCERT HALL SHAPERS

I think that acoustics are an exact science, whereas our perception of sounds
is a complex cognitive science. We should not mix up one thing with another.

—Paul Andru

Since the coupled tunable shell had resolved many of the symphonic acoustic problems associated with the older vaudeville and
movie multipurpose theaters used by many orchestras throughout
the last century, it would seem that acousticians could take a well-
deserved rest.

But there is no rest for the weary. Although the coupled tunable
shell had solved many problems in older halls, it failed to do as much
for the large new multipurpose halls that were built from 1970 to
the present day. These halls were designed to present opera, ballet,
and Broadway musicals as well as concerts and were built with huge
stage houses 90 feet (27 meters) tall, with a volume of 500,000 cubic
feet (14,158 cubic meters).

Two conditions related to these new designs reduced the effectiveness of coupled shells. The large volume of these stage houses
reduced the sound level of coupled energy returning to the audience chamber, and the new local opera and ballet companies took to

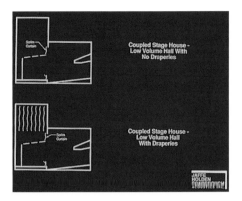

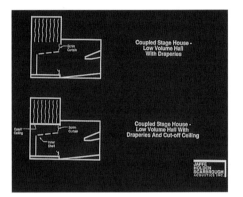

storing their absorptive scenery in the very location we were counting on to couple volume. In effect, the hard coupled space of the smaller vaudeville and movie houses was replaced with a large absorptive volume of stored scenery and house draperies. Not only was the coupling effect negated, but the direct orchestral sound energy was lost in these fly spaces.

This was the cue for the entrance of the concert hall shaper. Having had such success with coupled shells in theaters and music pavilions with small stage houses, I deduced that if I could reduce the volume of these large stage houses by introducing a heavy intermediate ceiling in these spaces, I could once again place the orchestra in a coupled shell within a 200,000-cubic-foot (5,663-cubic-meter) volume of air.

It was in Tokyo that the design received its name. At a meeting of the design team with the Tokyo Municipal Government (TMG), I mentioned that we would be developing a design concept that included a shell within a shell. This struck an unfamiliar chord, and a member of the TMG group, concerned about finances, asked, "Dr. Jaffe, why is it that most acousticians require only one shell in a theater and you are advocating two?" I was stumped. Our meetings were all held in Japanese, and I wasn't sure that a complicated technical answer would suffice. Luckily, I was saved by our Japanese associate consultant, Kawakamisan of Yamaha Acoustic Research Laboratories. He immediately responded by saying, "There is only one shell; the second device is actually a concert hall shaper." Since no one in the room, including me, had ever heard the term before, the answer was readily accepted with a bow or two and the acoustic team was on its way.

The basic shaper consists of a massive ceiling positioned by electromechanical winch systems. The shaper ceiling must have the acoustic characteristics of a regular concert hall ceiling in order to contain bass energy. Mounted on the upper surface of the ceiling are winches that control the tunable coupled shell ceiling panels and concert lighting fixtures mounted on the underside of the unit.

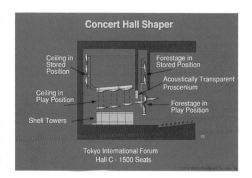

Once in position, the ceiling stretches from fly gallery to fly gallery at a height of 40 feet (12 meters). All scenery and house drapes are stored in the volume above the shaper ceiling. The standing towers of the shell are stored in a nested configuration in the stage wings when not in use. The tower units have variable grilles installed in the surface faces to further increase coupling capability.

The first shaper was designed and installed at Hall C, a 1,500-seat multiuse concert hall in the Tokyo International Forum. The intermediate ceiling unit was built by Mitsubishi Heavy Industries. The towers were mounted on motorized go-carts and could be whipped around the stage like bumper cars, a design that speeded up the erection process but added to the anxiety of any pedestrian onstage at the time.

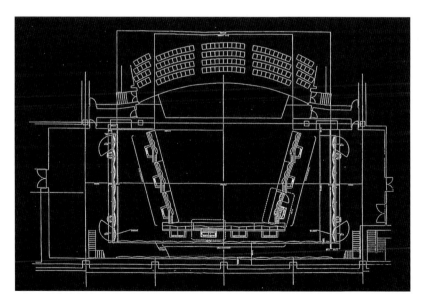

Plan of concert shell and shaper at Hall C, Tokyo International Forum, Tokyo, Japan. Architect: Rafael Viñoly. Acoustics: Jaffe Holden Scarborough.

THE ACOUSTICS OF PERFORMANCE HALLS

The second application of the shaper was a more sophisticated design for the Bass Performance Hall in Fort Worth, Texas. The side towers had adjustable grilles cut into the face of the units, so we could adjust the size of the openings incrementally for the best coupling characteristics.

Thelma Gaylord Performing Arts Theatre, Oklahoma City, Oklahoma. The second concert hall shaper in the western hemisphere. Architect: Polshek Partnership. Acoustics: Jaffe Holden Scarbrough.

Bass Hall was designed as a traditional European opera house with horseshoe balconies and a domed ceiling. However, we made sure that the upper balconies were strictly decorative technical spaces so we might develop a proper hard cap to the room, one of the secrets to the success of all concert halls and music pavilions. In my opinion, the most important ingredient that the shaper at Bass Hall brings to the acoustic cocktail is the volume of air surrounding the orchestral platform, which replicates the halls noted for the most favored traditional concert sound and eliminates harshness and stridency.

The hall opened in 1998 to extremely favorable reviews from the national music press and was acclaimed by the Cleveland Orchestra and the New York Philharmonic when they performed in the venue. For a more detailed description of how the shaper functions, see Case Study of Bass Hall at the end of this chapter.

The next concert hall shaper was installed at the Thelma Gaylord Performing Arts Theatre in Oklahoma City. Hall C, Bass Hall, and the Gaylord Theatre all received outstanding responses to their symphonic acoustic environments.

LESSONS LEARNED

FORESTAGE CANOPY

To enhance acoustic presence, intimacy, and clarity in wide halls or music pavilions that have limited side-wall coverage, one must design a series of reflectors forward of the proscenium arch over the orchestra pit and, at times, even farther out into the house. However,

Tokyo International Forum, Tokyo, Japan. Entertainment and convention center incorporating four theatre venues. Architect: Rafael Viñoly. Acoustics: Jaffe Holden Scarbrough.

we found that we had to be careful as to how far out these reflectors were positioned and also how dense a pattern one should employ. If the reflectors are placed too far beyond the stage and the pattern is too full, a reduced amount of energy will be transferred to the upper hard cap of the listening area and the loudness of the reverberation will be reduced in relation to the direct sound of the orchestra. We first encountered this problem in Hall C at the Tokyo Forum and again at Bass Hall in Fort Worth.

In Tokyo, architect Raphael Viñoly won the competition for the Forum project by placing four square buildings of progressively

Tokyo International Forum, Hall A, Tokyo, Japan. Five-thousand-seat symphonic concert hall utilizing ERES technology. Architect: Rafael Viñoly. Acoustics: Jaffe Holden Scarbrough.

THE ACOUSTICS OF PERFORMANCE HALLS

smaller sizes opposite an elongated building on the other side of a large open court. The design team lovingly called the project "four boxes and a banana." The first and largest box enclosed Hall A, a 5,000-seat multiuse concert hall. The next-smaller box housed a large conference center and the third, a still smaller box, held Hall C, a 1,500-seat multiuse concert hall with natural acoustics for musical presentations.

Since the boxes were getting smaller and smaller down the line, the required volume for symphonic presentation forced the shape of Hall C into a towerlike configuration (remember, one sets the volume of a concert hall on the basis of the power of the performing group, not on the seating capacity). Placing a forestage canopy with a full ceiling configuration over the pit and beyond gave us difficulty in generating sufficient levels of reverberation in the hall. The sound was very good and well liked, but the ratio of reverberant to direct sounds was somewhat lower than we had planned for the orchestra seating area.

We could of course position the orchestral string sections out on the pit, but this would reduce seating capacity, and in the very competitive booking climate among halls for orchestral concerts in Tokyo, this was not considered an option by management. Another solution would be to create some openings in the forestage ceiling and enable more energy to reach the cap of the room.

In Fort Worth, a somewhat similar situation arose during rehearsals for the opening. I had designed three individual forestage canopies forward of the arch and all was going well. However, I felt that the reverberation levels in the orchestra seating area were on the low side. I mentioned this to Ernest Fleischmann, executive director emeritus of the Los Angeles Philharmonic, who was visiting the facility at the time. "Take out the last canopy," he suggested. I did, and the level of reverberant sound in the orchestra section immediately blossomed. It was the sound I was striving for. I had gone on the assumption that if two canopies were good, three would be better. I had forgotten the lesson learned at the old Philharmonic Hall at Lincoln Center. A limited number of reflectors forward of the orchestra did wonderful things for the sound at Tanglewood, but covering the entire hall with reflectors, as was done at the New York hall, was not such a good idea.

A technique that can be used to increase the level of reverberation when designing new multipurpose concert halls works best for intermediate-size halls of 1,800 people or thereabouts. We call it "Cab Forward" in our studio, and I discuss it in Chapter 13.

Nancy Lee and Perry R. Bass Performance Hall

An innovative acoustical design concept enhanced a multipurpose hall's versatility and flexibility at the Nancy Lee and Perry R. Bass Performance Hall. It's rare, to say the least, that multipurpose performance halls earn kudos from top orchestra conductors. But after the New York Philharmonic played in the then-new Bass Performance Hall in Fort Worth, Texas, in 1999, Maestro Kurt Masur pronounced its acoustics "perfect" and lauded Bass Hall as being "among the top halls in the world."

Can you truly design a multiuse hall with "perfect" acoustics? Many of those who have played or listened to orchestral performances in such venues might find such a judgment dubious, for it's an old truism that multipurpose halls are no-purpose halls and do not provide the required acoustical environment for any type of performance.

For decades, architects and acousticians have struggled to find an effective way of supporting the very different acoustical demands of orchestral concerts, operas, rock-and-roll acts, or Broadway-style musicals within the same space. Solutions that have been attempted include averaging acoustic criteria, in the belief that each art form would prosper even though the acoustic environment for each one was quite a bit off-kilter; introducing variable absorptive draperies in the audience area of a reverberant space to enhance speech intelligibility; moving solid ceilings up and down to adjust air volume and thus vary reverberation times; and installing "demountable" orchestral shells in the stage house. Although these efforts improved the acoustical environment for some events, such as amplified programs of musical theater and popular performance artists, they never truly succeeded in providing the traditional symphonic sound for orchestra and opera performances. In addition, many of these solutions were very expensive and suffered from technical drawbacks that made them difficult to deploy and seriously restricted the speed with which the stage crew could convert the space from one purpose to another.

Theater owners and managers are very well aware that unwieldy "solutions" can have a devastating effect on the bottom line by limiting a house's flexibility. This is especially true in smaller cities, where adequate municipal and private funding for operating costs may be hard to obtain. In communities where one multipurpose venue must play host to a wide variety of performances, it is critically important that the hall be rapidly adaptable to those different uses. Scheduling—making sure the auditorium is being used as often as possible—is the key to economic viability. The imperative to fully book a theater is especially strong when a performance hall is home to a number of local nonprofit companies such as symphony orchestras, opera companies, and dance groups that don't pay market rates for using the hall. In those cases, the hall's managers must attract a large number of revenue-generating touring events in order to survive.

If a demountable orchestral shell takes too long to set up and strike, it may not be possible to schedule the number of performances, rehearsals, and touring events needed to keep the hall in the black. Economic viability might also be endangered if, for example, storing an orchestral shell requires so much fly space that the venue can't readily accommodate the sets needed for a touring Broadway-style show—meaning that a road company might have to bypass that venue.

So what makes the 2,100-seat Bass Hall—besides its acoustic suitability for orchestral concerts—so successful? One major factor

Nancy Lee & Perry R. Bass Performance Hall, Fort Worth, Texas. Note vertical grilles in shell towers that open to the coupled volume of the chamber. Architect: David Schwartz. Acoustics: Jaffe Holden Scarbrough.

is that it incorporates our innovative concert hall shaper, which has proven to be extremely versatile in terms of its operational capabilities. According to Bass Hall's former managing director, Paul Beard, the shaper has ensured the auditorium's fiscal health by enabling it to schedule 200-plus performances of every type—not to mention rehearsals and private parties—per year. "We have a building that's fully occupied, continuously productive," he says. "It's a fantastic base for amortization."

The key feature of the concert hall shaper is a secondary acoustic ceiling deployed in the stage house at a height of 40 feet (12 meters) above the stage deck. This ceiling, which stretches from one side gallery to the other, connects the volume contained under its surface to the volume of the audience chamber, creating a one-room concert hall for classical music presentations. When the ceiling is moved back into storage position against the theater's upstage wall, the hall is transformed into an outstanding venue for opera and ballet. Deploy the variable draperies on the side walls of the audience chamber and the acoustics of the hall provides a proper environment for amplified musical theater and popular music productions such as country and western, rock and roll, and jazz.

Deployed, the shaper closes off the upper reaches of the stage house, where house dressing and scenery are stored. Integral to the shaper's ceiling design are individual tunable ceiling sections that incorporate orchestra reading lights and that are lowered into position by winches mounted on the upper surface of the shaper itself. The side towers of the enclosure are rolled into position on dollies from storage locations in the wings. These towers have variable grilles, or openings, that, together with the tunable ceiling sections, allow acoustic energy to flow from the stage enclosure to the shaper volume and back again.

To work effectively, the shaper must be complemented by volume in the audience chamber sufficient to meet the acoustic criteria required for symphonic performance. The energy developed under the shaper ceiling should be added to the *overall reverberation* of the hall and should not create a source-identifiable late-arriving aural decay (as would happen if the shaper were installed in a room having a low reverberant field in the audience area). Increasing the

Nancy Lee & Perry R. Bass Performance Hall, Fort Worth, Texas. BELOW LEFT: *Section showing the location of drapes used to lower reverberation for amplified popular music programs and Broadway theater.* BELOW RIGHT: *Section showing the concert hall shaper. Architect: David Schwartz. Acoustics: Jaffe Holden Scarbrough.*

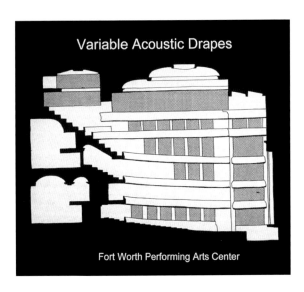

Variable Acoustic Drapes

Fort Worth Performing Arts Center

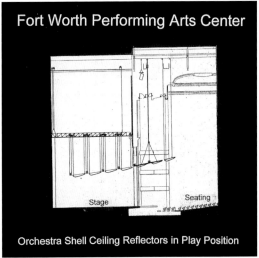

Fort Worth Performing Arts Center

Stage   Seating

Orchestra Shell Ceiling Reflectors in Play Position

Nancy Lee & Perry R. Bass Performance Hall, Ft. Worth, Texas. Erection shot of concert hall shaper with sound transparent proscenium masking curtain. Architect: David Schwartz. Acoustics: Jaffe Holden Scarbrough.

loudness of the reverberant energy creates a better ratio between the direct orchestral energy and that of the reverberant field, especially in the orchestra seating area and on the stage platform itself. The success of this approach depends on coupling the shaper's volume to an adequate audience-chamber volume.

When the ratio between these volumes is carefully calibrated, and the correct balance between direct and reflected sound achieved, the concert hall shaper can produce an acoustic quality in a multi-purpose hall that is equal to or even better than that of the world's best single-purpose-built concert halls. This is especially true onstage and in the rows closest to the stage. Sophisticated classical music fans have long recognized that the front rows of the orchestra are often the worst seats in a single-purpose concert hall. The late dean of New York music critics, Harold Schonberg, for example, would never sit closer than thirteen rows from the stage in Carnegie Hall and other venues, because the high level of direct orchestral sound tends to mask the reverberant room ambiance and reduce the blend and balance of the ensemble. The coupled volume of the concert hall shaper, on the other hand, by increasing the sound level of mid- and

Nancy Lee & Perry R. Bass Performance Hall, Ft. Worth, Texas. Side-wall towers moving into position under tunable shell ceiling reflectors. Architect: David Schwartz. Acoustics: Jaffe Holden Scarbrough.

low-frequency reverberation in both the early and the late decay fields and by balancing the strings to the brass and percussion sections through the use of tunable ceilings, provides listeners in seats

THE ACOUSTICS OF PERFORMANCE HALLS

close to the stage with an aural environment that is balanced between the early direct and the later-arriving reflected sound fields—an environment equal to the best locations in the house. This means that the concert hall shaper can make the experiences of concertgoers throughout the house equally enjoyable—as well as improve the quality of the sound heard by the musicians onstage.

In addition to providing sufficient volume in the stage house, we designed three canopies forward of the proscenium arch to further enhance early reflections in the hall and to act as orchestral ceilings at those times when the orchestra was set forward on the orchestra pit lifts. (This might be required at a concert with the 300-member Mormon Tabernacle Choir). During our tuning procedures, we discovered that, as in Tokyo's Hall C, the third forestage reflector (the one farthest from the stage) cut off too much orchestral sound from the orchestra when the ensemble was located in its normal position behind the proscenium arch. Thus, we suggest that designers make sure that sufficient orchestral energy always be allowed to reach the upper "cap" of the audience chamber.

Beyond conferring concert-hall-quality acoustics on multipurpose halls, the concert hall shaper provides two other benefits that improve upon the performance of conventional orchestral shells: it takes up much less space when stored, and it can be assembled and struck much more easily.

When placed in the storage position, the shaper's ceiling doesn't block a single line set in the fly space. By contrast, the component ceilings of a conventional tunable shell are typically flown from existing line sets attached to the grid. When ceilings are stored that way, the thickness of each ceiling, combined with that of the attached symphonic down light fixtures, results in the loss of two to three line sets *per ceiling*. Since an orchestra with chorus requires four ceilings for proper sectional balance, grid-flown orchestral shells can take up as many as twelve line sets.

This will create big problems when a hall is scheduled to host a touring Broadway show, a fully staged opera, or a theatrical extravaganza like Cirque du Soleil or Riverdance, since productions like these usually require every one of the sixty or so line sets in a typical proscenium theater. It is possible to remove the ceilings from the fly space and temporarily store them in a trailer for the duration of the theatrical production. However, that can be a lengthy and costly procedure and may not be doable within the necessary time frame. In addition, it may not be cost-effective if the traveling show is staying in town for only a few performances.

The other great advantage of the concert hall shaper is the speed with which changeovers can be done. The crew at Bass Hall can accomplish the transformation from symphony set to open stage house in one and a half to two hours—which makes it possible, theoretically, to schedule an orchestral rehearsal in the morning, a ballet rehearsal in the afternoon, and a symphony performance that same night. Since the ballet scenery and prefocused lighting fixtures were previously stored in the fly space above the shaper ceiling, all the crew has to do is let in the lines for the ballet sets once the shaper is safely stored against the back wall of the stage house following the end of the symphony rehearsal. The process is reversed to get ready for the evening orchestral event.

If, indeed, we have added sufficient volume to the audience area of Bass Hall and made sure the upper part of the room has a hard cap, how do we handle the acoustic environmental needs of other events such as opera, ballet, and amplified popular entertainment? Once the shaper is removed from the stage, the proscenium opening becomes a large absorptive surface. Adding this absorption with curtains that can be drawn in niches in the hall itself, the reverberation times are reduced for good natural and amplified speech intelligibility.

When you compare this added expense to the extra revenue that a hall can realize over the years through continuous bookings, the amount becomes insignificant; the concert hall shaper is a very sound investment.

THIRTEEN

CAB FORWARD

Ms. Wu and Mr. Finckel, the society's artistic directors, should promise
audiences that every future concert will keep the hall's stage fully extended,
despite the loss of seats. Who would have thought that Tully Hall could feel
that intimate?

—Anthony Tommasini

Several years ago, Chrysler introduced a line of cars that they
called Cab Forward, which featured increased space in the passen-
ger cabin. When I needed a name for a new acoustic approach to
provide the traditional concert hall environment, I settled on Cab
Forward as a good descriptive name, because in these designs the
strings and woodwinds are positioned forward of the proscenium
arch in the listening area of the room.

In previous chapters, I discussed how acoustical designers could
develop a proper source area for musicians and audiences in a multipurpose hall utilizing a tunable orchestra shell. One approach
was to couple the volume of the shell with that of a hard low-vol-
ume stage house in older vaudeville and movie theaters. Another
was to create a similar volume backstage in a music pavilion and
couple it to a tunable shell. When the stage-house volume of new
multiuse theaters became too large, cutting off the upper volume

at 40 feet (12 meters) with a concert hall shaper yielded similar successful results.

But how should an acoustician handle a new commission in a community that might find the costs of the shaper technology beyond their means, or in a situation in which the architect determines that the structural design might not accommodate such a device? Here is where Cab Forward can save the day. What we recommend in these instances is to build the orchestra pit lift large enough to seat the string and woodwind sections of the orchestra and develop the architectural design of the listening area of the room forward of the proscenium as if it were a part of the orchestra shell. In addition, one must install at least two canopies over the pit extension to enable the musicians sitting on the pit to hear themselves and other members of the ensemble.

Several segments of a tunable shell are still needed behind the arch for the brass, percussion, and chorus. Since the brass and percussion sections (as well as a chorus when used) are the most high-powered groups in symphonic performances, their sound will come through the arch without any problem. This arrangement

Weidner Center for the Performing Arts, University of Wisconsin, Green Bay, Wisconsin. Sketch illustrating the design of the cab forward concert hall. Architect: Beckley/Myers. Acoustics: Jaffe Acoustics.

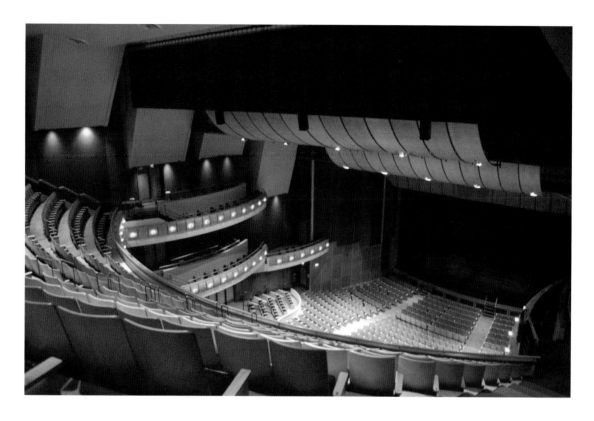

automatically provides a good balance among the strings and wood-winds sitting on the pit lift and the brass, percussion, and chorus located on stage behind the arch.

For smaller ensembles and soloists who do not require as long a reverberation time, one might lower the orchestra pit lift and place all the musicians in the normal position on the stage. The wall and ceiling pieces of the shell that is used to reinforce the brass, percussion, and chorus in the full-orchestra setup can be used here for the smaller ensembles and soloists.

Is there a downside to this approach? Well, sort of. Cab Forward does not work well in halls with more than 2,200 seats. In a multi-use hall where symphonic events are presented on stage, the theater consultant must set the auditorium sight lines to the front edge of the stage (assuming that Romeo and Juliet just might die on the floor at

Cofrin Family Hall of the Edward W. Weidner Center for the Performing Arts on the campus of the University of Wisconsin, Green Bay, Wisconsin. Note how the design of the side wall and overhead reflectors forward of the proscenium replicate the surfaces of an orchestra shell. Architect: Beckley/ Meyer Acoustics: Jaffe Acoustics.

the stage lip). By moving an orchestra out on a pit lift, the sight-line point is moved about 25 feet (7.6 meters) forward, pushing back the rear balconies and steepening the rake of all seats in those areas. In a large-capacity hall, this places many patrons at quite a long distance from the action when opera, ballet or theater companies stage their productions behind the arch (25 feet or 7.6 meters more, to be exact). Many theater consultants object to using this approach in halls seating 2,400 to 3,000 people.

In addition, it can prove difficult to use Cab Forward in an existing hall, since the side walls of the listening area are not designed to accommodate the string and woodwind sections and there are no overhead reflectors over these sections to project sound and enable the musicians to hear themselves. When we held evaluation rehearsals of Cab Forward at Detroit's Orchestra Hall and Avery Fisher Hall at Lincoln Center, the musicians were very uncomfortable playing forward of the proscenium without overhead reflector support.

Is there a solution for these existing halls that may not be structurally strong enough to support a concert hall shaper or fitted out to handle Cab Forward? The answer is yes, and the next chapter describes how one can handle these situations.

FOURTEEN

ELECTRONIC ARCHITECTURE

It is time that those of us who care about orchestras admit that perhaps we are not doing things in the best possible way, and to examine alternatives. Are we willing to open our minds to completely new practices and behaviors? I certainly hope so.

—Henry Fogel

Of all the innovations I have developed to enhance the presentation of symphony orchestras—the tunable coupled shell, the concert hall shaper, the tubular cardboard shells, and Cab Forward—it was electronic architecture, otherwise known as Electronic Reflected Energy Systems (ERES), that presented the most opportunities for orchestras to have acoustically excellent and economically sound concert halls. Electronic architecture has nothing to do with reproducing or reinforcing the orchestral sound. It is a technique for creating reflections essential to producing the traditional European concert hall sound in a room or an outdoor environment that is not physically able to produce them.

When I began to design electronic systems that would reproduce physical sonic reflections, I coined the term Electronic Reflective Energy Systems (ERES) to distinguish these designs from the standard reinforcement systems being used to amplify performances. The basic technique of ERES is to pick up the direct natural sound of the orchestra with one or two microphones suspended from the ceiling of the hall about 10 feet (3 meters) forward of the stage platform. This sonic information is then isolated into three separate channels, digitally processed to reproduce reflecting patterns that match those in widely acclaimed venues such as Boston's Symphony Hall, and reintroduced into the space through loudspeakers located throughout the room. The electronic processing of the original direct sound accommodates variables that affect the strength and frequency characteristics of reflections, such as materials of hall construction, air absorption, distance of listener from stage platform, ceiling height, and under-balcony configuration.

If a room is too wide for audience members to receive the early reflections needed for intimacy, presence, and transparency, ERES will furnish these reflections 20 or 30 milliseconds after the arrival of the direct sound from the stage. In effect, the system will make the room aurally narrower. If the air volume of a room is too low in relation to the absorptive factors, or the reverberation times at mid and low frequencies are inadequate, ERES will provide the ongoing reflections needed to extend the reverberation in the hall to the amount required throughout the frequency range. These physical changes in the acoustic environment may be thought of as raising the ceiling electronically.

Does it really work? The Indianapolis Symphony has been using such a system in their concert hall, the Hilbert Circle Theatre, since 1984, and the Milwaukee Symphony has had an installation in place at the Marcus Center since 1997. At the opening of the renovated Circle Theatre, John Nelson, music director emeritus of the Indianapolis Symphony, said, "The sound is as good as that in any hall I've been in." And in Milwaukee, guest conductor Mitch Miller reported: "I just did three concerts with the Milwaukee Symphony. . . . The concerts were sold out and they went bananas at the beautiful sound."

Uihlein Hall, Marcus Center for the Performing Arts, Milwaukee, Wisconsin. Stage area after renovation showing new ceiling canopy. Original architect: Harry Weese Associates. Acoustics: Kirkegaard Associates. Shell Design Jaffe Holden Scarbrough, ERES design: Christopher Jaffe/David Robb.

I was not the first to think about re-creating reflections in a concert hall that was deficient in mid-frequency reverberation, although I was the first to realize that other important reflective energy criteria, such as initial time delay gap and warmth, could also be introduced into spaces as required, and I hold a patent for integrating three-channel ERES systems with tunable reflectors in a concert hall. Early pioneers in this field were Harry Olson of RCA, John Ditamore of Purdue University, Peter Parkin of the Building Research Station in the United Kingdom, and Paul Veneklasen, the noted American acoustician. Early efforts in the 1930s did not have the advantage of modern low-distortion equipment, but nonetheless great progress was made. Olson made use of tubular delay lines by sending sound down a tube and reintroducing it electronically at a later time depending on the length of the tube. Ditamore and Veneklasen used external reverberation chambers—small, hard rooms where long reverberation times could be developed and then reintroduced electronically into the concert hall. Parkin developed a unique system called Assisted Resonance (AR) that utilized a multiplicity of small physical resonators to create the needed reflections.

It was Parkin and his group at the Building Research Station in London who developed AR specifically for the improvement of Royal Festival Hall in London, a concert hall built in the late 1950s that was extremely deficient in reverberation at both mid and low frequencies. The hall was continually criticized by musicians and critics until the Parkin AR system was installed in the early 1960s. Since

Royal Festival Hall, London, England. The organ, behind the doors over the choral seating, elevates the reflectors away from the stage platform. Architect: London County Council Architectural Department. Acoustics: Hope Bagenal with Building Research Station.

"electronics" is a naughty word in the classical music business, the installation was accomplished with great secrecy, and those involved were cautioned on pain of death to tell no one of the installation.

Two amusing things occurred as a result of the conspiracy. Herbert von Karajan, the conductor of the Berlin Philharmonic, who had been a vocal critic of Festival Hall after it opened, brought his orchestra to London to perform in the room after the installation of AR had been completed. He was quite pleased with the symphonic environment on that occasion and told the press that there had been a great improvement in the acoustic characteristics of the room. He attributed this to the fact that the original plaster had finally dried out—one more example of myths and legends in concert hall acoustics.

Another story involves critic Harold Schonberg. In the early sixties, he went to London to find out what the hullabaloo was about in terms of the improvements to Festival Hall and reported back after his first night at the hall that the sound was magnificent. Later that week, emulating the CIA, he found out that the electronic AR system had been installed, and he complained in his next review that he had been duped; the sound wasn't really as good as he had first thought. (Schonberg several years later raved about the electronic architecture systems that I had installed in Indianapolis, Indiana, and Eugene, Oregon.)

One might ask the question, if acousticians can physically copy the acoustic characteristics of shoebox halls, reproduce required natural reflection patterns in rooms of different geometry, and successfully adapt tunable shells and concert hall shapers in multiuse halls, why should we even consider using ERES, particularly when the musical community is opposed to it?

For starters, ERES can be the only solution available in terms of improving an existing hall that is not a candidate for a major renovation. Old film and vaudeville houses with deep under-balcony areas and low air volume, such as the Circle Theatre in Indianapolis or the Majestic Theatre in San Antonio, Texas, were good candidates for this technique. The buildings could not have been used for classical performances without the addition of ERES; the Circle Theatre in Indianapolis would have been torn down if the symphony had not become its owner.

New multiuse halls in communities that have a limited number of symphonic performances or a tight budget can also benefit from the applications of ERES. With this technique, the costs of a concert hall shaper and motor-operated variable absorption are eliminated. From an architectural design standpoint, the options are unlimited, since acousticians no longer have to integrate key natural reflection patterns into an architectural scheme. The appearance of a hall does not change from symphony concerts to opera performances to rock-and-roll events when you no longer need to drop curtains or other absorptive material into the space.

Circle Theatre Concert Hall, Indianapolis, Indiana. A vaudeville theatre–movie palace converted to a concert hall. Architect: Dalton, van Dijk, Johnson & Partners. Acoustics: Jaffe Acoustics.

THE ACOUSTICS OF PERFORMANCE HALLS

Tokyo International Forum, Hall A, Tokyo, Japan. Concert hall with glass side walls. Architect: Rafael Viñoly. Acoustics: Jaffe Holden Scarbrough.

Examples of this design approach in new construction are the concert venues in Eugene, Oregon, and Anchorage, Alaska, and the 5,000-seat Hall A at the Tokyo International Forum. In both Eugene and Anchorage, electronic architecture freed the architectural firm of Hardy Holzman Pfeiffer to develop interior designs incorporating

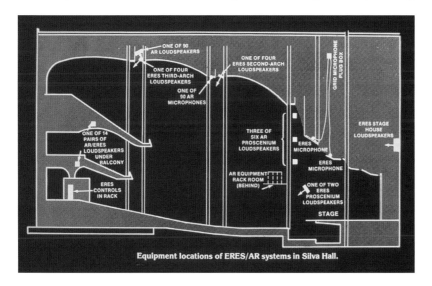

Equipment locations of ERES/AR systems in Silva Hall.

Hult Center for the Performing Arts, Eugene, Oregon. An ERES multipurpose hall that does not require variable acoustic draperies. Architect: Hardy Holzman Pfeiffer Associates. Acoustics: Jaffe Acoustics.

indigenous motifs such as Indian basket weaving and the aurora borealis respectively in these venues. In Hall A in Tokyo, we were able to assist architect Rafael Viñoly to achieve his vision of a concert hall with illuminated translucent glass side walls.

We have seen how electronic architecture can improve the concert environment in rooms not particularly well suited for symphonic performances, and now this same technique can be used in multiuse halls.

A third application for ERES is in the lawn areas of music pavilions such as Ravinia Park in Illinois, and open-air concert sites such as Central Park in New York and Millennium Park in Chicago. Since there are no reflections out of doors, these systems can provide the required aural information to simulate indoor spaces.

Older musicians and conductors are wary of electronic manipulation. They have been burned by poor microphone placement techniques during recording sessions and subjected to inexperienced

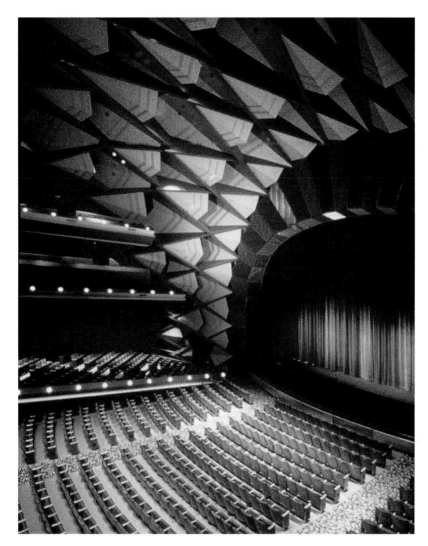

Evangeline Atwood Concert Hall, Anchorage, Alaska. Another multipurpose hall utilizing an ERES concert hall system. Architect: Hardy Holzman Pfeiffer Associates. Acoustics: Jaffe Acoustics.

sound-mixing operators at outdoor concert venues. At times, inadequate sound reinforcement equipment has plagued them during al fresco concerts. They do not trust the mixing board operators, who can change sectional balances as well as overall orchestral dynamics during recording sessions, pseudoconductors interfering with their interpretation of the music. In an article in the *New York Times* in 1975, conductor Lorin Maazel was not very complimentary in his remarks about recording engineers who "haven't the talent to become conductors and who like to twirl knobs and play God."

Conductors do have a few valid reasons to be upset. Poor microphone placement may not pick up all the overtones of an instrument or may allow the sound of other instruments to enter sound-mixing channels devoted to reinforcing other sections of the orchestra. When the console operator decides to lift the violas, he may inadvertently bring up the trumpets and the trombones as well.

There was, and still is, a tremendous prejudice against the use of these electronic systems in concert halls and a total misunderstanding of how ERES actually functions. Overcoming these prejudices was a difficult task. Although I completed a number of successful ERES installations that received wonderful reviews from the critics and complete acceptance from the clients using the facilities, this work became a handicap in terms of obtaining new concert hall commissions. Potential clients dismissed my work designing well-received natural acoustic halls and music pavilions and considered me a pariah when it came to maintaining the purity of musical presentations. Frustrated by this turn of events, I began to look for a way to convince the musical community that ERES enhances the listening experience for both the musicians and their audiences and, when designed correctly, is indistinguishable from sound energy reflected from the walls and ceilings of a concert hall.

My opportunity came in the early seventies after Nancy Hanks, an executive at the Rockefeller Brothers Fund, was named the first chairperson of the National Endowment for the Arts (NEA). Ms. Hanks was a brilliant administrator and an innovative thinker who was able to convene the most talented artists in America to work on her panels.

Knowing of Ms. Hanks's interest in the application of new technology in the arts, I applied for an NEA research grant through the West Virginia Arts Council (now Commission). The goal of the research was to develop a method to obtain graphic signatures of well-received natural acoustic halls that could be compared to the signature of a hall that had been enhanced through the design and installation of an ERES system. Ms. Hanks believed that this study would be of value to orchestras throughout the country and gave me the green light (as well as the green money) to go ahead.

Several acousticians, including Peter Parkin at Festival Hall, had already presented graphic measurements illustrating that reverberation could be successfully extended electronically, so I chose to measure and compare the graphic reproduction of early lateral reflections from Carnegie Hall in New York City and the Corson Auditorium at the Interlochen Center for the Arts in Michigan with those at the Ravinia Pavilion, a fan-shaped music pavilion with no side walls. A year earlier, we had installed an ERES early field channel at Ravinia to improve presence and clarity. The objective was to see if we could match the natural early lateral wall reflections of the well-liked venues with lateral reflections produced by ERES loudspeakers in the indoor-outdoor venue. Two of my associates in our office at the

William Lobb of Jaffe Acoustics checking the sound source at the Ravinia Festival Music Pavilion during the National Endowments for the Arts concert hall research study. Participants: Christopher Jaffe, William Lobb, Louise Fryman.

time, William Lobb and Louise Fryman, worked with me on this project; the late Julius Bloom, manager of Carnegie Hall; Roger Jacobi, president emeritus of the Interlochen Arts Academy; and the late Edward Gordon, executive director of the Ravinia Festival, gave us permission to take measurements in their halls and provided us with stagehand assistance in setting up the experiments.

In order to record early lateral reflections, we placed a dodecahedron loudspeaker (a twelve-sided spherical ball with a loudspeaker in each of the twelve segments) on the stage to simulate the sound projection of a symphony orchestra. The sound from these speakers was full frequency and omnidirectional, simulating the patterns one might expect to hear emanating from the stage during an orchestral concert.

In the auditorium, we positioned a microphone pointing into the center of a parabolic reflector that was mounted on a camera swivel stand. The microphone was connected to an oscilloscope that gave us a graphic representation of reflections coming from specific portions of the wall surfaces. The microphone was positioned halfway between the stage lip and the balcony rail, the location recommended for measuring the initial time delay gap (which determines the famous clarity and intimacy criteria). The patterns were generated by an electronic pulse fed into the loudspeaker onstage.

The three-member research team traveled to New York City; Grand Traverse Bay, Michigan; and Highland Park, Illinois, to take the required measurements. At Ravinia, the outdoor facility, we measured lateral energy with the system on and off. The test results were very gratifying. The ERES system was able to perfectly duplicate the lateral wall reflections from the two indoor concert halls.

The successful results of this research enabled many symphonic organizations to reconsider the application of ERES in their halls. Many have had ERES systems designed to reproduce the environment of the great concert halls of the world and installed in their

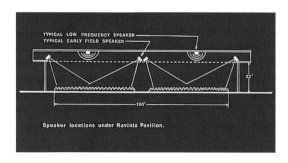

Speaker locations under Ravinia Pavilion.

home symphonic venues. Major orchestras, such as the previously mentioned Indianapolis and Milwaukee symphonies, have used ERES for many years, as have lower-budget orchestras such as the San Antonio, Eugene, and Anchorage symphonies. One would hate to think that the prejudices of a conductor, executive director, or music critic might prevent audiences as well as musicians from enjoying the benefits of an outstanding environment for the presentation of symphonic music.

My position is that if an existing concert hall for a major orchestra can be acoustically improved through physical means for a reasonable amount of money ($10 million to $25 million), such a renovation program would be worth the expenditure. However, if the cost exceeds this amount, the parties involved might be advised to look into an electronic enhancement solution.

Chicago Symphony rehearsing at the Ravinia Festival Music Pavilion. Highland Park, Illinois. Architect for the renovation: Holabird and Root, Acoustics: Jaffe Acoustics.

A lower-budget orchestra might consider ERES from the start. The cost of a typical system is under $500,000, and the money for a physical renovation might be better spent on musicians' salaries, top-flight soloists, and the commissioning of new works.

In some instances, such as the Circle Theatre in Indianapolis, the physical impossibility of raising the ceiling to gain volume in a landmarked building led us to a combination solution of limited physical changes with electronic enhancement. In Milwaukee, the opera company was so well pleased with the acoustics of Uihlein Hall for *their* needs that they objected to any physical changes in the hall that might improve the environment for the symphony. Here we combined changes to the stage shell with an electronic solution.

We have experienced projects in which a city wants to build a multiuse facility for a broad number of local classical arts companies as well as for major moneymaking traveling events. In this instance, the symphony may plan to present only eight or ten concerts a season. Should the owners go to the expense of a full-blown symphonic-style multiuse hall with a concert hall shaper or a Cab Forward treatment, or should they consider electronic enhancement? It would be worth their while to carefully examine all options.

If the Indianapolis Symphony can use ERES for twenty years, maybe electronics enhancement in a symphony hall isn't the devil's work after all.

Speaker locations at Oakland Paramount Theater, Oakland, California.

From the early analog ERES system I designed for the Paramount Theatre in Oakland, California, in the early seventies to the sophisticated digital systems being built today by LARES, Yamaha, Meyer, ACS, and SIAP, ERES has achieved more and more acceptance. Now that ERES is used in many American concert halls as well as opera houses all over the world, younger classical musicians, brought up in a world of electronic miracles, are much more willing to consider the use of these systems to enhance the acoustic environment of symphonic and operatic performance venues.

LESSONS LEARNED

ERES—ELECTRONIC REFLECTED ENERGY SYSTEMS

The earliest lesson learned about ERES was that musicians, music critics, and administrators are very prejudiced against using these systems in concert halls and will sometimes sacrifice audience enjoyment rather than utilize this very effective tool. Since I believed it was my responsibility to create the best possible acoustic environment for the presentation of symphonic programs in any room so designated, I sometimes offered ERES as a solution in certain projects where it was impossible or impractical to attempt to produce the Europea traditional sound through physical means alone because of structural, programmatic, or financial considerations.

When a conductor is replaced in one of these facilities, it is an excellent idea for the acoustician to hop on a plane and meet with the new conductor prior to his taking over the podium to explain the reasons why this approach was taken and how the system operates. It is also important to keep in close touch with orchestra management where these systems are in use in order to make sure they are still tuned as designed or to determine if they are in need of maintenance. On occasion, the symphony and hall administrators argue as to who should maintain these systems, and we have experienced situations in which financial impasses of ridiculously small amounts result in systems being shut off.

An interesting point concerns the duplication of the traditional sound. The time arrival of early and late reflected energy is balanced against the direct sound emanating from the musicians. Is the manipulation of these criteria within these architectural design limits the most emotionally satisfying sonic experience available to listeners? Is it possible that more reverberation can be tolerated, even desired, if the level of early reflections can be increased? In a natural hall, we will never know. In an ERES hall, one can experiment with balances and find out if a more exciting symphonic sound can be developed.

In reality, most of the musical community has been extremely pleased for us just to tune ERES systems to reproduce the traditional symphonic sound in all portions of the hall. The tight budgets of most orchestras preclude much experimentation. However, I have created some dramatically different symphonic sonic experiences in the anechoic chamber at the Rensselaer Polytechnic Institute's Architectural Acoustics Program.

The Concord Pavilion

The Concord Pavilion was the second surround outdoor music facility I designed. The first one, the Forum at Ontario Place in Toronto, was a perfect circle with amphitheater seating and the orchestra located at the center. The building, sited on the shores of Lake Ontario, was a tensile membrane structure without any side walls, which gave many patrons a clear view of the lake. There is a wonderful story about Seiji Ozawa (then the conductor of the Toronto Symphony), the Forum, the Canadian Navy, and the *1812 Overture*. Tradition has it that the armed forces of a country should supply actual cannon fire for the ending of Tchaikovsky's piece celebrating the Russian victory over Napoleon when it is played on a national holiday. This was the case at the Forum when Ozawa was conducting the Toronto Symphony for a holiday concert with destroyers of the Canadian Navy anchored offshore a mile away. The Navy was to fire the cannon shots when Ozawa whipped out a white handkerchief at the appropriate moment in the score, since the open side walls gave the sailors a clear view of the conductor's podium. Unfortunately, the maestro forgot that sound waves travel a great deal slower than light. Ozawa flashed the handkerchief at the exact moment he wanted to hear the cannons fire. However, as thunder takes a bit of time to follow a distant lightning flash, it was five seconds before the patrons in the hall heard the cannons fire (through air, sound travels roughly 1,130 feet per second, or a mile in five seconds). The booms of the cannons coming in five seconds late muddled the score for the ending, but nobody really cared. The destroyer fire was a surprise ending, and everyone could appreciate the fact that the light display from the cannon fire, instead of the sound, was timed to the music.

In addition to intimacy, the open side walls played an important physical acoustic role as well: they did not give echoes an opportunity to form and interfere with the direct sound from the stage and subsequent reverberation.

The physical and aural intimacy of the Forum is one of its best features, and John Toffoli, Jr., director of parks and recreation for the City of Concord, California, who was in the process of planning a music pavilion for the San Francisco Symphony, wanted to create the same ambiance in his facility. However, the full-circle design did not seem to be the best model for the Concord. The Forum was part

Ontario Place, Toronto, Canada. Exterior of the multimillion-dollar entertainment center on the shore of Lake Ontario. Architect: Zeidler Partnership. Acoustics: Jaffe Acoustics.

THE ACOUSTICS OF PERFORMANCE HALLS

of a larger overall city-sponsored entertainment and cultural center, and there was no charge for admission to the complex or to Forum events—even Toronto Symphony concerts were free to the public. Seating was on a first-come, first-served basis, and people wandered into the seating area from every direction. The Concord Pavilion program, on the other hand, was to be modeled on the typical eastern symphony pavilion operational style. Patrons would be charged admission and would be looking for all the amenities of a theater space, e.g., comfortable reserved seats, easy access to the facility from the parking lots, food and drink service nearby, and a sufficient number of restrooms.

When the planning of the Concord Pavilion began, I had already been selected as acoustician, because I had been working with the City of Concord for many years on an annual jazz festival that was

Ontario Place Pavilion, Toronto, Canada. Interior of the first surround symphonic music pavilion. Architect: Zeidler Partnership. Acoustics: Jaffe Acoustics.

held at a local park. In view of my ten years of experience working on music pavilion projects and my theatrical experience in New York City in the late forties and fifties, Toffoli asked me to handle the theatrical consultation work as well. Since the program differed from that of the Forum, I suggested we design a thrust stage surrounded by a 280-degree seating area instead of a full-circle hall. The building would accommodate 3,500 patrons under the roof, with choral seating behind the stage platform and a promenade behind the seats. A relatively steep lawn would encompass the building on three sides with good sight lines for 7,000 people sitting on the grassy slope.

The next step was to select an architect, and Toffoli interviewed a number of architects who had recently designed successful eastern music pavilions, including Meadow Brook, Saratoga, Merriweather Post, the Mississippi River Festival, and Blossom Center. At

Concord Pavilion (now Sleep Train Pavilion), Concord, California. San Francisco Symphony rehearsing on the center stage. Architect: Frank O. Gehry. Acoustics: Jaffe Acoustics.

THE ACOUSTICS OF PERFORMANCE HALLS

that time, Frank Gehry, who had designed the Merriweather Post Pavilion for the National Symphony with the firm Gehry, Walsh & O'Malley, had decided to set up his own firm in Santa Monica, California, and had had some disappointing experiences going to interviews at the offices of potential clients. He was convinced that that he had a unique way of designing buildings, which incorporated shed roofs and inexpensive construction materials such as corrugated sheet metal and chain-link fences. He sometimes referred to himself as the "cheapskate architect," not a name you could call him now. When clients came to his studio, he had a chance to show them how his studio functioned and take them to buildings that he had designed in the Los Angeles Basin using his unique architectural approach.

Gehry refused to come to Concord to be interviewed, and Toffoli was about to eliminate him from the competition when I interceded on Gehry's behalf. I had great respect for all the other architects on the list, particularly Peter van Dijk and Larry Medlin, with whom I had worked on the Blossom Center and the Mississippi River Festival respectively. However, I thought it important that Gehry have a chance to do a building in his home state and I persuaded Toffoli to meet Gehry in Santa Monica. The result is history: Gehry got the job and came up with a design that we might call ecologically sound today. The pavilion and the lawn area were sunk into a large bowl in a hillside surrounded by a 15-foot (4.6-meter) high earth berm. One cannot see the pavilion from the road or the surrounding area. When you walk through the entrance gate, it is like the moment Dorothy lands in Oz. You move from the sepia of the summertime hills to a green lawn and a colorful open pavilion environment. The relatively steep lawn and the berm keep pavilion program noise in and automotive noise out.

As I have described, one of my key acoustic principles when designing a music pavilion is to eliminate all balconies and create a hard cap in the upper portion of the room using the roof and side walls of the seating area above the height of 18 feet (5.5 meters). This

box or caplike volume provides the reverberation needed to create the
traditional orchestral sound in the shed area. Gehry, however, wanted
the roof to be a thin plane with no side walls whatsoever around
the audience seating. I called this his "Uneeda Biscuit" approach.
(As I have already noted, Frank Gehry and Malcolm Holzman are
the two architects who throughout my career have challenged me at
every turn; and frankly, I have enjoyed the opportunity to develop
new ways to provide traditional sound and give these architects a
chance to realize their vision for the space. I do not consider such
collaboration an acoustical compromise but a win-win-win situation
for the client, the architect, and the acoustician.)

The question, of course, was how to create the natural traditional sound without a hard cap to the room. A moat might help

improve bass response for those seated near the stage but could not create the level of mid- and low-frequency reverberation needed for 3,500 patrons. The only solution available was to create the traditional sound with an Electronic Reflected Energy System, which would produce the proper amount of reflective energy needed to create the sound. Again, bear in mind that such a system does not reinforce the orchestra but furnishes the reflections required to create the traditional European orchestral sound. The only commercial system available at the time was the English AIRO system developed by Peter Parkin for Festival Hall, London, and after a number of evaluation visits I and the client made, we settled on using it.

The concept worked well. Gehry had his thin roof; I had

Concord Pavilion, Concord, California. Architect: Frank O. Gehry. Acoustics: Jaffe Acoustics.

delivered the traditional sound, and the client had an exciting, attractive, and sonically healthy facility. In addition, unlike in other pavilions, when we shut off the AIRO system, the sonic environment became much more suitable for amplified popular entertainers, the groups that bring in the most revenue for these facilities.

FIFTEEN

ART AND ARCHITECTURE:
WILL THE TWAIN MEET?

Sooner or later we shall achieve what will be known as the SALLE [hall, auditorium], cathedral of the future, which, in a free, vast and flexible space, will bring together the most diverse manifestations of our social and artistic life.

—Adolphe Appia

Although it is now possible to design more informal concert halls that have an egalitarian approach in terms of the physical and emotional relationships between performers and audiences, the actual symphonic performance protocol has not really changed. Even in surround halls, audiences must sit as quiet as church mice and not clap between movements or at moments in the score that reach emotional high points. Conductors of major symphonies rarely address patrons, and the formal wear of the musicians and some patrons can cast a funereal pall over the entire evening.

Back in the 1960s and '70s, there seemed to be a breath of fresh air entering a number of venerable and staid concert halls. The Los Angeles Philharmonic concert with Frank Zappa, the New York Philharmonic Rug Concerts, and the 100,000-person Central Park Great Lawn concerts seemed to indicate a loosening of the collar stays.

What happened? Did the conservative backlash to the flower children affect performance styles as well as politics? It's a possibility.

However, I am pleased to report there is a fresh wind blowing in this country, and it is being felt from coast to coast.

At the Brooklyn Academy of Music, the administration has introduced a program called "Takeover," where younger audiences take over the various stages and lobbies of the building for an event that runs from 9 p.m. to 4 a.m. at a cost of only $15 a ticket. The program, inaugurated on November 3, 2007, featured bands, movies, DJs, and art installations. Granted, orchestral concerts didn't enter into the mix of this particular happening, but a reporter's survey found that many of the participants had been to the Brooklyn Academy only rarely or never. Several said they planned to return. Claudia La Rocco, reporting in the *New York Times* two days later, quoted Lisa Mallory, the Academy's vice president, the night of the "Takeover": "I'm not sure what this means, whether it's a good thing or not, but it's a reality that arts institutions must be thinking about. What will the performing arts be like in 10 to 20 years? I can't imagine that the formal sit-down for two and a half hours will be the only way to do it."

In the same article, Ms. La Rocco discusses how Peter Gelb is refashioning the Metropolitan Opera by screening free live telecasts of the opera on Lincoln Center Plaza and Times Square, and the Joyce Theater is updating its SoHo satellite to create a flexible space that artists can refashion as their work dictates. It is her opinion that tension exists between art and the structures in which it is performed, and, with time and financial success, organizations become more conservative and programs become static.

On the West Coast, the Simón Bolívar Youth Orchestra from Venezuela created a sensation at San Francisco's Davies Symphony Hall by programming a Shostakovich symphony with a medley of Latin American pieces and playing them sensationally well. During the performance of the Latin works, orchestra members snapped their fingers and shouted "Mambo!" at appropriate times. Individual players and even sections leaped to their feet to sway and dance with their stand partners.

At the end of the concert, the musicians left the stage, returning for an encore dressed in jackets decorated with the Venezuelan flag. All of this information was reported by Heuwell Tircuit, former music critic for the *San Francisco Chronicle*, who wrote, "In fifty years of covering orchestral concerts on four continents, I have never encountered anything close to such unlikely musical splendor."

What does this all mean? Having broken the tradition of the formal rectangular hall, are we now breaking up the new tradition of the surround hall, and if so, what is the next symphonic performance venue going to look like? Although court masques of old encouraged eating, drinking, and gossiping as part of the evening's experience, I doubt that all audiences will enjoy the more sophisticated scores of the classical repertoire being performed in a noisy, distracting environment.

It is my thought, observing symphonic performances at music pavilions such as Tanglewood, Ravinia, and Blossom Center, that people select the listening environment best suited to their needs. Those wishing to totally envelop themselves in the aural experience sit in fixed rows inside the pavilion, concentrating on the score and the technical virtuosity of the musicians. Those more inclined to think of the concert in broader terms spread out on blankets on the lawn, sip wine, partake of artisanal cheese, and soak up the music over the low background hum of crickets in the woods.

Considering the great popularity of these events as well as those symphonic concerts presented at the Hollywood Bowl and on the lawn at Central Park, I believe that the next step in the evolution of concert halls will be a building that I call the indoor music pavilion.

Several years ago, Peter van Dijk, architect for Blossom Music Center, and I developed some plans for an indoor music pavilion. The shape of the room would be somewhat like the conical form of Blossom, and classical music would be presented *au naturel*. The fixed seating area would surround a thrust stage in a 190-degree pattern. This would ensure physical and aural intimacy for all patrons. At the rear of the pavilion would be an indoor lawn covered with

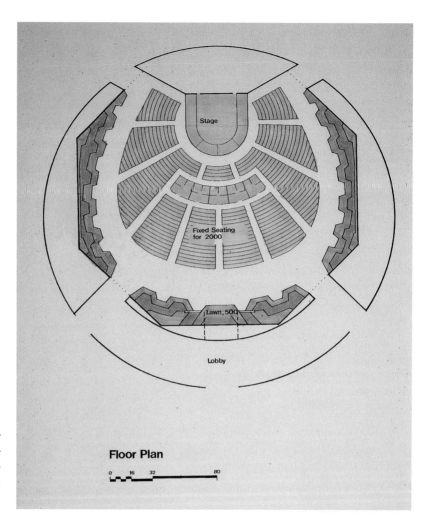

Stage

Fixed Seating
for 2000

Lawn, 500

Lobby

Floor Plan

0   16   32   80

Plan of proposed Indoor Pavilion. Architect: Peter van Dijk. Acoustics: Christopher Jaffe.

carpet that would provide all the amenities associated with outdoor lawns, sans crickets.

There would be no formal stage house, but a certain amount of winch-operated rigging would enable modern dance companies, unit-set operas, and amplified popular entertainers to share the stage with classical music artists. Since the building would be designed to symphonic acoustic standards, we would have to add some variable absorption in the space.

Section of proposed Indoor Pavilion. Architect: Peter van Dijk. Acoustics: Christopher Jaffe.

Today, new 2,000-seat, one-purpose concert halls are being budgeted at between $130 million and $350 million, depending on how much titanium you use. A 2,200-seat indoor music pavilion could be built for $50 million to $60 million, excluding land costs.

The indoor pavilion is just one concept; I'm sure there will be many more as the need for less formal performance spaces becomes evident to the musical community, the architect, and the theater consulting professions.

Adolphe Appia, the famed nineteenth-century scenic and lighting designer who worked with Wagner at Bayreuth, had a vision for the theater of the future quoted at the beginning of this chapter. It is our responsibility to see that his vision is realized.

WHAT TO DO UNTIL
THE DOC ARRIVES

There are a great variety of concert hall acoustic diseases. The good news is that none of them are fatal if you are willing to accept the latest medical procedures as well as alternative medicine. Arthroscopic surgery is out, as well as herbal draughts, but lots of other solutions may apply. Just as women, men, and children have to be treated separately, so different categories of orchestras must be handled accordingly.

Here are my thoughts on how one might set up categories at the beginning of an examination:

- What type of building is the orchestra performing in? Is it a one-room concert hall, a new multiuse concert hall—theater, a renovated movie palace or vaudeville house, a music pavilion, an outdoor band shell, etc.?
- What is your financial condition? Do you have health insurance, or have you dropped through the safety net? We must know if you can afford treatment at the Mayo Clinic or whether the chewing-gum-and-string approach must suffice. Perhaps you have a rich uncle who will come to the rescue. If so, please note on admission form.
- How open are you to various types of treatment? A Christian Scientist might refuse to go on life support, and a skeptical scientist might pass on ginseng roots.

- Who is really in charge of making decisions regarding your treatment? Have you signed a living will giving the conductor, the musicians, the administration, the board, or all of the above the decision-making power of resuscitation?

Now you know who you are. The next step is to determine where it hurts, and so we must ask you to describe your symptoms.

- "Doctor, it's my lower frequencies. Every time we play Tchaikovsky, my brass and percussion blow my lower string notes away. I can see those bows moving, but I can't hear a thing. Don't they make mutes for those big horn things?"
- "Doctor, I'm in an amateur orchestra. My Aunt Sadie comes to every concert and sits in the center orchestra seating area of our hall. She continually claims there is a veil between her and the sound of my ensemble. Is it possible that enemy aliens have placed a force field between her and the stage?"
- "Doctor, the musicians in my ensemble are very difficult to deal with. They are constantly complaining that they can't hear one another, and I'm at my wit's end. I can't afford risers, and the conductor says that monitor speakers are out. When you come, don't forget your crystal ball."
- "Doctor, the air-conditioning system in our hall does not work well. If we turn it on, it blows the pages of our music off the stands, and when we turn it off, we are fined as an unlicensed sauna. I don't think Mozart had this problem."

Although the symptoms listed here seem a bit over the top, they are, in fact, typical of the problems faced by hundreds of orchestras around the country. Orchestras performing in major metropolitan centers, rural communities, conservatories, and high schools can all experience these conditions. Although this is not a workbook, I can offer some assistance.

SOME REMINDERS ABOUT IMPROVING ORCHESTRAL BALANCE AND ONSTAGE HEARING

Most balance and onstage hearing problems appear when an orchestra is playing in a multiuse proscenium theater of one sort or another—e.g., a new multiuse venue, an existing or renovated movie palace or vaudeville house, or a high school auditorium. Earlier wisdom suggested that all the orchestral energy behind the proscenium arch in these theaters should be captured and directed at the audience. This approach failed to take orchestral balance and onstage hearing into consideration. The power level of a double bass is 0.16 watts, while the power level of a trombone is 6 watts and a bass drum is 25 watts. For this reason, it is essential that we reduce a portion of orchestral energy at the rear of the orchestra platform where these high-powered instruments are located. Listed below are a number of ways this can be accomplished in a variety of stage settings.

Contained Orchestra Shell

Cut openings into the rear wall of the shell as well as the ceiling of the shell closest to the rear wall. These openings can be masked using metal grilles backed with some lightweight cloth material. You would not want to use sound-transparent grille cloth because backstage lights might shine through. Additional reduction in brass and percussion sound can be achieved by bringing the upstage drapery traveler onstage directly behind the open grilles or by spraying the rear wall of the shell with a light coat of acoustical material.

This type of shell may already improve orchestral balance since there are open spaces between the individual ceiling panels. However, should the problem persist, it is possible to either raise the upstage ceiling panel (the one over the brass and percussion) or angle it in such a manner as to allow more energy to escape into the flies. Here again, bringing the upstage drapery onstage or bringing a teaser in near the opening between the rear wall and the last ceiling can help the situation.

No Shell

Obtain a tunable shell with independent ceiling panels from one of the many shell manufacturers. If funds are a problem, you can build one in a high school or local woodworking shop with wood frames and doped canvas. Carnegie Hall used canvas ceiling pieces over their stage from the 1940s until a major renovation was completed in the 1980s.

All of the above solutions should aid onstage hearing and orchestral balance.

As to Aunt Sadie and her force field, fly a lightweight ceiling canopy forward of the proscenium arch so that early reflections will reach her in time. (An electronic forestage canopy might also be employed.)

If your problems are related to the forced air system, contact a local mechanical engineer to evaluate your system. Hopefully, the problem can be readily and economically resolved.

CREDITS

INDEX

Erratum

The caption on page 96 should read:

The Concertgebouw, Amsterdam, The Netherlands. With 20 percent of the audience surrounding the musicians, this hall can be considered the precursor of modern surround concert facilities. Architect: A. L. van Gendt.

ERRATUM

These credits are missing following page 204: